THE OFFIC
MANCHESTER
UNITED
QUIZ BOOK

Compiled by John White

Foreword by
ALEX FERGUSON CBE

DEDICATION

This book is dedicated to my mum and dad,
my wife Janice and our two sons, Marc and Paul

ACKNOWLEDGEMENTS

Firstly, I would like to say a special thank you to my wife, Janice, for painstakingly
proof reading the book for me. I would also like to thank all of my family and
friends who encouraged me to compile this book, Deborah and Nicky at
André Deutsch for helping to ease the book through for publication and everyone
at André Deutsch for making my dream come true. Finally, a special word of
thanks is reserved for the *Boss*, Mr Alex Ferguson, for writing the foreword for
this book, a man for whom I have nothing but the utmost respect and admiration.

First published in Great Britain in 1998 by Manchester United Books
an imprint of André Deutsch Ltd
76 Dean Street
London W1V 5HA

www.vci.co.uk

André Deutsch Ltd is a VCI plc company

10 9 8 7 6 5 4 3 2 1

Printed and bound by Butler and Tanner, Frome and London

A catalogue record for this book is available from the British Library

ISBN 0 233 99419 X

Designed by Design 23
Photographs from Colorsport and Popperfoto

Foreword

It is a pleasure to write a few words at the start of John White's Official *Manchester United Quiz Book*. He has spent over a year researching the questions (and answers!), and I am delighted that his labours have now been rewarded in print. John has excellent credentials for compiling this book – not only has he been a United fan for all his 35 years, but he has travelled regularly to Old Trafford from his home in Northern Ireland to see his heroes perform. He now has a season ticket in the Stretford End and makes the journey across the Irish Sea for every home match – fantastic dedication.

John was also responsible for forming the Carryduff Branch of United's Supporters Club in 1991, and it is now one of the largest in Ireland with 300 members. All the members of the Branch have been superbly loyal to me and my backroom team during my managerial career with United, and I take this opportunity to thank them all for their magnificent support.

Quizzes seem to be becoming increasingly popular in a day and age when statistics are analysed more than ever before (perhaps too much!). Fantasy Football seems to be the 'in' thing and no longer is the game just about goals, but assists, clean sheets and times of substitutions as well. Apparently, the latter can affect the points your selected players achieve!

As a result of John's efforts a donation will be made to research into Muscular Dystrophy, a cause that I have become personally involved with during recent months. Thank you for making your own contribution towards the work.

I hope you get as much pleasure from the hours of pondering these questions as I know I will!

ALEX FERGUSON CBE
Manager, Manchester United FC

Preface

This book was compiled to allow Manchester United fans all over the world to test their knowledge about the World's Greatest Club. The questions take you back to the early days of the club, when they were known as Newton Heath, and bring you up to the 1997-8 season. They bring back memories of the 'Glory Years' in the club's long and proud history as well as remembering the sad times, such as the Munich air disaster of 1958. The questions are a trip through time, a trip that I hope you enjoy making. And for the Expert Reds, there is a special section to fully test your advanced knowledge.

I have made every effort possible to ensure that the answers are correct but should any answer be incorrect, I beg your forgiveness in advance. I hope you enjoy the book as much as I enjoyed compiling it and researching the many questions that United fans have posed me.

To United fans everywhere, keep the spirit of 1958 alive and *Come on You Reds.*

J.W.

CONTENTS

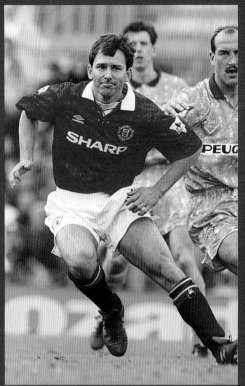

1 DOUBLE WINNERS 1993-4

1. Who did United knock out in the Fourth Round of the FA Cup?

2. Old Trafford's largest attendance of the season was 44,751. Can you say who the visitors were?

3. Which team completed a league double over United during the season?

4. United's biggest league win of the season was at Old Trafford on 16 March 1994. What was the score and who were the opposition?

5. During the season United drew 11 of their 42 league games. What was the most common score, 1-1, 2-2 or 3-3?

6. Peter Schmeichel was sent off in the Sixth Round of the FA Cup at Old Trafford and replaced in goal by Les Sealey. Name United's cup opponents and the player who was substituted for Sealey.

7. United's biggest away win in the league was against a Greater Manchester rival. Can you name the team United hammered 5–2?

8. Name the only player to have played in all 42 of United's league games.

9. Who was the top goalscorer for the Reds in the league?

10. Two players, who are no longer with the club, scored for United in the 3-2 home win over Oldham Athletic on 4 April 1994. Can you name them?

ANSWERS ON PAGE 140

2 OLD TRAFFORD

11. The first ever League Cup Semi-Final replay was staged at Old Trafford in 1961. Can you name the two teams involved?

12. How many Group games did Old Trafford stage during the 1966 World Cup Finals, 2, 3 or 4?

13. United's first-ever match at Old Trafford took place on 19 February 1910, but the Reds failed to celebrate the occasion with a win. Which team spoilt their big day?

14. Which Cup Final replay did Old Trafford stage in 1911?

15. To the nearest 5,000 can you say what United's record league attendance is at Old Trafford?

16. In what year after the Second World War did United play their first FA Cup tie at Old Trafford?

17. United welcomed their first foreign visitors to Old Trafford in 1951 for a fixture organised to celebrate The Festival of Britain. Who did United play?

18. In 1970 Old Trafford staged its third FA Cup Final. Can you name the two teams involved?

19. Name the Scottish club who were ordered by UEFA to replay a European Cup Winners' Cup tie with Rapid Vienna at Old Trafford on 12 December 1984 following trouble at their own ground.

20. Old Trafford staged a Cup Final in consecutive years during the 1970s. Can you name the Cup and the years concerned?

ANSWERS ON PAGE 140

3 GENERAL – ROUND 1

21. To the nearest 50,000, can you say how many fans attended league and cup games at Old Trafford during the 1993-4 season?

22. Which United player, wearing the No.9 shirt for England against West Germany at Wembley on 23 February 1966, scored the only goal of the game?

23. Can you name the goalkeeper who saved an Eric Cantona penalty during a Premier League game in April 1997?

24. What event took place at Old Trafford on 25 March 1957?

25. In the Manchester league 'Derby' at Maine Road on 13 March 1974, a player from each side was sent off, Mike Doyle for the Blues and which United player?

26. Can you name United's Lancashire rivals whom they defeated 2-1 at Old Trafford on 7 April 1956, effectively clinching the Championship for the Reds?

27. Which club was the first to beat United's very successful Youth Team in the FA Youth Cup?

28. United lost only one league game at Old Trafford during their 1964-5 Championship-winning season. Who were the successful visitors?

29. Can you name the Midlands club United thrashed 7-0 in a league match on 8 April 1970 ?

30. Which team did United beat 1-0 on 5 April 1975 and thereby secure a return to the First Division, and subsequently win the 1974-5 Second Division Championship?

ANSWERS ON PAGE 140

4 PICTURE QUIZ – ROUND 1

1. Brian McClair has a nickname at Old Trafford, do you know what it is?

2. Brian headed United's winner in a Coca-Cola Cup Quarter-Final replay in 1994. Who were the opposition that day?

3. Can you name the Midlands club where Brian was an apprentice during the 1980-1 season?

4. Prior to the start of the 1996-7 season Brian scored in two consecutive friendlies for United in a tournament hosted by Nottingham Forest. Against which two clubs did he score?

5. Who were the opposition for his Testimonial at Old Trafford in March 1997?

ANSWERS ON PAGE 140

5 EUROPEAN CUP WINNERS' CUP

31. How many times have United taken part in the ECWC?

32. Can you name the United player who scored an own-goal against Barcelona on 7 March 1984 in the Nou Camp?

33. Who were United's first-ever opponents in the competition?

34. Which team knocked United out of the 1985-6 competition ?

35. In the 1990-1 ECWC how many of their nine games did United actually lose ?

36. Name the United player who scored twice against Barcelona in the 1983-4 Quarter-Final second leg at Old Trafford.

37. True or False – Brian McClair scored in every round of the 1990-1 competition, including the Final ?

38. Can you name the two teams United beat home and away in the 1990-1 ECWC ?

39. On 5 October 1977 United had to play their First Round, second leg home tie away from Old Trafford because of crowd trouble in the first leg. Which ground did they play at and what team play their home games there ?

40. Name the English First Division club United beat in the Second Round of the 1963-4 ECWC.

ANSWERS ON PAGE 140

6 TRANSFERS – ROUND 1

41. Danny Wallace left United on 15 October 1993 to join a club from the Midlands. Can you name it?

42. From which club did United sign Lee Sharpe?

43. Who was the first player Matt Busby signed when he became United's manager?

44. Ted MacDougall joined United from Bournemouth for £200,000. Name the manager who signed him.

45. Prior to joining the Reds which club did Andrei Kanchelskis play for?

46. Tommy Docherty brought Gordon Hill to United from Millwall, but before he joined United, Hill had been on loan to a team in America. Can you name them?

47. From which club did United buy Jimmy Greenhoff?

48. Which Danish team did Peter Schmeichel play for before arriving at Old Trafford?

49. Can you name the Irish side United bought Pat McGibbon from?

50. Lou Macari left Old Trafford in 1984. Which club did he move to?

ANSWERS ON PAGE 140

7 INTERNATIONAL MIXED BAG – ROUND 1

51. Four United players appeared for Scotland in the 1978 World Cup Finals. Name them.

52. Name the two United players who represented a 'Rest of Europe' team in Scandinavia in 1964.

53. Can you name the United star who captained a 'Rest of the World' side against Great Britain in 1947?

54. Name the Yugoslavian international who played for the Reds in the 1980s.

55. Which United player played for a 'Rest of the World' team against England in 1963?

56. Norman Whiteside made his international debut in the 1982 World Cup Finals in Spain. Which country did he win his first cap against?

57. Only two United players won full international caps for Wales during the 1970s. Who were they?

58. Name the United defender who made his international debut for Scotland in 1973.

59. Name the three Danish internationals who have played for United.

60. Name four of the United players who were capped by the Republic of Ireland during the 1970s.

ANSWERS ON PAGE 140

8 PICTURE QUIZ – ROUND 2

1. Gary won a medal in his first season at Old Trafford. Which competition did United win?

2. During the 1992-3 season Gary scored only one Premier League goal. Against which team did he score?

3. Can you name the league club were Gary spent a while on loan from Middlesbrough?

4. What is Gary's registered height on the United books?

5. Pally scored three League goals during the 1996-7 season. Two of them came against Liverpool. Who else did he score against?

ANSWERS ON PAGE 141

9 MATCH THE TROPHIES WITH THE YEAR THEY WERE WON

61. Rumbelows League Cup Winners   1991

62. FA Cup Winners   1993

63. European Cup Winners' Cup Winners   1909

64. European Cup Winners   1992

65. Division 2 Champions   1936

66. FA Cup Winners   1952

67. Division 1 Champions   1911

68. European Super Cup Winners   1968

69. Premier League Champions   1991

70. Division 1 Champions   1963

ANSWERS ON PAGE 141

10 CHAMPIONS 1996-7 – ROUND 1

71. Prior to the start of the season Alex Ferguson paraded all five of his new summer signings. Name any four of them.

72. Name the United player who scored his first, First Team goal against Nottingham Forest in a pre-season friendly on 4 August.

73. A week before the season kicked off United beat Newcastle United in the Charity Shield. What was the score of the game and who were the United goalscorers?

74. Against which side did United register their first home win in the Premiership?

75. Eric Cantona missed his first-ever penalty for United in a competitive fixture on 7 September. Name the opposition.

76. Can you name the opposition when Raimond van der Gouw played his first Premiership game for the Reds?

77. Who scored United's last Premiership goal of the season and who were the visitors to Old Trafford?

78. Name the team United played twice in the space of only four days during November.

79. Who was United's goalscorer in the 1-0 win over Liverpool at Old Trafford?

80. Ole Gunnar Solskjaer was United's top goalscorer in the Premiership. How many league goals did he score?

ANSWERS ON PAGE 141

11 THE 1970s – ROUND 1

81. How many away wins did United record in the league during season 1973-4?

82. During the 1974-5 season, six players with a surname beginning with the letter 'M' appeared in United's league side. Can you name four of them?

83. How many appearances did George Graham make for United during the 1974-5 season?

84. Can you name the Midlands club that knocked United out of the FA Cup in the Third Round, during the 1972-3 season?

85. Name the United player, who with 13 goals, was the club's leading goalscorer for the 1979-80 season.

86. In season 1971-2 what was so unusual about United's opening two home league games against Arsenal and West Bromwich Albion?

87. Name the ground where United defeated Derby County in the FA Cup Semi-Final of 1976.

88. Can you name the two brothers who appeared together in United's team three times during the 1973-4 season?

89. Only one player appeared in all 42 of United's league games during the 1970-1 season. Can you name him?

90. Can you name the Yorkshire club United beat 5-1 at home and 4-1 away, during the 1975-6 season?

ANSWERS ON PAGE 141

12 PICTURE QUIZ – ROUND 3

1. Can you name this United legend who played for the club from 1906-21?

2. From which club did United sign him?

3. To aid concentration he used to play with something clenched between his teeth. What was it?

4. What nationality was he?

5. How many First Division Championship medals did he win with United?

ANSWERS ON PAGE 141

13 LEAGUE CUP – ROUND 1

91. Only two players started for United in all nine of their Coca-Cola Cup games during the 1993-4 season. Gary Pallister was one, can you name the other?

92. Can you name the Lancashire club that beat United 5-1 in the Second Round of the 1966-7 competition?

93. What scoring record does Alex Dawson hold for United in the League Cup?

94. Name the United player who scored in both legs of the 1970-1 Semi-Final.

95. Apart from Aston Villa, in the Final, which other team defeated United in the 1993-4 Coca-Cola Cup?

96. Can you name the Premier League side who knocked United out of the 1992-3 competition in Round Three?

97. Who scored United's goal in the 1983 Final?

98. Which player was United's top goalscorer in the 1993-4 Coca-Cola Cup with five goals?

99. United reached the Semi-Final of the League Cup in 1974-5. Who beat them?

100. Name the United player who was sent off in the 1994 Final.

ANSWERS ON PAGE 141

14 LEAGUE CHAMPIONS 1992-3

101. United didn't record their first win at Old Trafford in the league until 2 September 1992. Who did they beat?

102. Between 19 September 1992 and 24 October 1992 United drew five consecutive league games. Can you name three of the teams they drew with?

103. United got the season off to a bad start by losing their opening fixture. Name the club they lost to.

104. What team was the first to defeat United in the league in 1993?

105. Only three players were ever-present throughout the entire league campaign. Can you name two of them?

106. On Boxing Day 1992 United took part in a six-goal thriller, with the game ending in a 3-3 draw. Who were the Reds' opponents?

107. United's biggest league win of the season was a 5-0 win at Old Trafford on 28 December 1992. Can you name the unlucky visitors?

108. Who was top goalscorer in the league, Hughes, Cantona or Kanchelskis?

109. Old Trafford's largest league attendance of the season was 40,447, a match against a Lancashire rival. Name them.

110. Aston Villa finished the season as Runners-up to United. How many points did they finish behind the Reds, 8, 9 or 10?

ANSWERS ON PAGE 141

15 THE EUROPEAN CUP – ROUND 1

111. On 25 April 1957 United played their first-ever European tie at Old Trafford. The game ended in a 2-2 draw. Who were the opposition?

112. In the 1994-5 Champions League, Eric Cantona only played in two games. Can you say who he played against and whether it was a home or away tie?

113. United beat Kispest Honved 2-1 at Old Trafford on 29 September 1993. Name the United player who scored twice in the game.

114. Can you name the first side beaten by United in a European Cup tie at Old Trafford?

115. Three teenagers started for the Reds in their 1994-5 Champions League game against Galatasaray at Old Trafford. Name them.

116. Two United players with the surname beginning with the letter 'C' scored in the first leg of the 1958 European Cup Quarter-Final against Red Star Belgrade. Can you name both of them?

117. In the 1968 European Cup Final, who scored Benfica's equaliser which put the game into extra-time?

118. In what continent did United play Galatasaray when they visited the Ali Sami Yen Stadium, Europe or Asia?

119. By what nickname is the above Stadium better known?

120. What was the aggregate score, over both legs, when United beat Athletic Bilbao in the Quarter-Final of the 1957 European Cup?

ANSWERS ON PAGE 141

16 PICTURE QUIZ – ROUND 4

1. How many FA Cups did United win during Robbo's time at Old Trafford?

2. What record did he set whilst playing for England in 1982?

3. Against which team did he score his last competitive goal for United?

4. How did he create football history in 1990?

5. What did the training staff at West Bromwich Albion mix with Guinness to build him up in the early part of his career?

ANSWERS ON PAGE 142

17 CAN YOU NAME MY PREVIOUS CLUB? – ROUND 1

MATCH THE UNITED PLAYER WITH THE CLUB HE LEFT TO JOIN THE REDS

121. Mal Donaghy   Doncaster Rovers

122. Harry Gregg   Wolves

123. Gery Daly   Hull City

124. Jim McCalliog   Partick Thistle

125. David Herd   Tranmere Rovers

126. Paul McGrath   Everton

127. Stuart Pearson   Arsenal

128. John Gidman   St Patrick's Athletic

129. Alex Forsyth   Luton Town

130. Steve Coppell   Bohemians

ANSWERS ON PAGE 142

18 REARRANGE THE LETTERS TO FIND PAST AND PRESENT UNITED STAR

131. RAYOSNBOBRN   _ _ _ _ _ / _ _ _ _ _

132. CLTBEANOSLARN   _ _ _ _ _ _ / _ _ _ _ _ _ _

133. TCAINREAOCN   _ _ _ _ / _ _ _ _ _ _ _

134. KEEDARTOPB   _ _ _ _ _ / _ _ _ _ _

135. TBSYREIGLRRA   _ _ _ _ _ / _ _ _ _ _ _ _

136. RSALYPATEILGR   _ _ _ _ / _ _ _ _ _ _ _ _ _

137. BESTLOBSIYN   _ _ _ _ _ / _ _ _ _ _ _

138. EKRLARPAPU   _ _ _ _ / _ _ _ _ _ _

139. HARMSKHEUG   _ _ _ _ / _ _ _ _ _ _

140. DANACTERPR   _ _ _ / _ _ _ _ _ _ _

ANSWERS ON PAGE 142

19 MATCH THE PLAYER WITH THE CLUB UNITED BOUGHT HIM FROM

141. Terry Gibson

Tottenham Hotspur

142. Noel Cantwell

Burnley

143. Martin Buchan

Sunderland

144. Alan Brazil

Sheffield Wednesday

145. Chris Turner

Coventry City

146. Albert Quixall

Brentford

147. Mike Phelan

Aberdeen

148. Willie Morgan

Leeds United

149. Stewart Houston

Norwich City

150. Peter Barnes

West Ham United

ANSWERS ON PAGE 142

20 PICTURE QUIZ – ROUND 5

1. United signed me from Shamrock Rovers in October 1986. Who am I?

2. Under which United manager did I make my debut for the club?

3. I left United in a £275,000 transfer in November 1988. Which club did I join where I tasted relegation, defeat in the play-offs and finally, promotion?

4. What happened to me on my first Full Team debut?

5. Where in Ireland was I born?

ANSWERS ON PAGE 142

21 UNITED IN EUROPE – ROUND 1

151. In which European city did United win the 1991 European Cup Winners' Cup?

152. Name the Russian side that knocked the Reds out of the 1992-3 UEFA Cup.

153. Who is United's all-time top goalscorer in European competition?

154. What number did George Best wear on his shirt in the 1968 European Cup Final?

155. United met Real Madrid in the Semi-Final of the European Cup in 1957. What United record was set in the away leg?

156. Can you name the United player who was sent off in the 1994-5 Champions League game in Gothenburg?

157. In the 1984-5 UEFA Cup United met a Scottish team. Can you name them?

158. United have met two English club sides in European competition. Can you name both of them?

159. In their 1992-3 UEFA Cup games United used three substitutes. Bryan Robson was one of the players whilst the other two were defenders. Name them.

160. Two players, who were part of the 1968 European Cup winning team, survived the Munich Air Disaster. Who were they?

ANSWERS ON PAGE 142

22 WHO AM I? – ROUND 1

161. I cost United a club record fee of £825,000 in August 1979. I won 84 caps for my country and an FA Cup Winner's medal with the Reds in 1983.

162. I made my United debut when I was only 16 and went on to play over 200 league games for the Reds. In 1983 I scored in two different Wembley Cup Finals.

163. Prior to signing for United, in a £1.5 million deal in June 1989, I had played for Reading and Portsmouth. When I left the Reds in 1992 I returned to another former club.

164. In 1991 I was named PFA Young Player of The Year and won a ECWC Winners' medal. In 1992 I added a League Cup Winner's medal to the latter.

165. I was a Scottish international who cost United £200,000 in January 1973. During the 1970s I won an FA Cup Winner's and two Loser's medals with the Reds. I left United in 1984.

166. Before joining United in August 1989 I was already an England Under-21 international. A medical problem almost prevented me from moving to Old Trafford, however the problem was not as serious as had initially been diagnosed.

167. Born in 1973, United snapped me up from Manchester City's School of Excellence in July 1990. I made my debut for the Reds against Everton and won my first international cap for my country against Germany in 1992.

168. I cost United £1 million in 1992 and after only three games for the Reds I broke my leg. When I left United I joined another Premiership club.

169. I made my United debut in September 1963. I won two Championship medals with the Reds and in 1968 won The Football Writers' Association Footballer Of The Year Award.

170. Matt Busby gave me my first international cap. I joined the Reds on 12 July 1962 for £115,000 and went on to play almost 400 games for the club, scoring 236 goals in my 11 years at Old Trafford.

ANSWERS ON PAGE 142

23 GENERAL – ROUND 2

171. Which player won the PFA Young Player of the Year Award in 1994?

172. Which United player did Japanese side, Grampus Eight, reportedly want to sign in November 1991?

173. Can you name the United player who became the first player for 11 years to be sent off for Wales in November 1990?

174. *The Good, The Bad and The _ _ _ _ _ _* can you complete the title of this autobiography and name the United player who wrote it?

175. Name the two players whose heated confrontation ended in a fight on the pitch at Old Trafford when United met Arsenal in a league game in 1990.

176. During which season did United first compete in the UEFA Cup?

177. Two players with the same surname as a country in South America have played for the Reds. Can you name them?

178. Name the team United thrashed 5-1 at Old Trafford in the Third Round of the Coca-Cola Cup during the 1993-4 season.

179. Which United player scored his 100th goal for the club in the Rumbelows Cup Final of 1992?

180. Can you name the United official who in 1968 said, 'When spacemen reach the moon I wouldn't be surprised if they found George Best's boutique there.'?

ANSWERS ON PAGE 142

1. How many times did George finish the season as United's top goalscorer?

2. In 1970 George was sent off when playing for Northern Ireland against Scotland. For what reason was he ordered off?

3. During the 1979-80 season George played for a Scottish Premier League side. Can you name them?

4. Between the 1969-70 and 1973-4 seasons, how many goals did Best score for the Reds in European games?

5. In what year during the 1980s was George sent to prison, 1981, 1985 or 1989?

ANSWERS ON PAGE 143

25 FA CUP – ROUND 1

181. United, the Cup holders, were on the receiving end of a Cup upset when they crashed out of the 1983-4 competition at the first hurdle. Can you name the side that beat them in the Third Round?

182. United drew neighbours City in the Third Round on 10 January 1987. Who scored the only goal of the game, for the Reds?

183. Between the 1989-90 and the 1995-6 competitions, United's earliest exit from the Cup took place during the 1991-2 season. Can you name the team that beat United at Old Trafford in the Fourth Round?

184. Name the United forward who scored five goals in the 8-0 mauling of Yeovil Town in the Fifth Round on 12 February 1949.

185. United's first game at Old Trafford after the Munich Air Disaster was a Fifth Round FA Cup tie on 19 February 1958. United won the game 3-0 but who did they beat?

186. Name the London club United defeated 5-3 at Highbury in the 1958 Semi-Final.

187. Can you name the Irish striker who scored in the last minute of the game against Everton at Old Trafford in the Sixth Round of the 1982-3 competition?

188. Who were United's opponents in the 1979 Semi-Final?

189. United beat Bristol City 1-0 in the 1909 Final, United's first FA Cup win. Where was the match played?

190. Which club beat United 1-0 in the 1966 Semi-Final at Burnden Park, Bolton?

ANSWERS ON PAGE 143

26 DOUBLE DOUBLE WINNERS – ROUND 1

191. United's highest home league attendance of the 1995-6 season was 53,926. Who were the visitors?

192. United were at home in the Third Round of the FA Cup and drew the game 2-2. Who scored for the Reds?

193. Which team did Paul Parker score against in an FA Cup tie in January 1996?

194. Which one of the Neville brothers started the 1996 FA Cup Final?

195. Name the player who played the most Premiership games for the Reds during the 1995-6 season.

196. At which ground did United play Chelsea in the FA Cup Semi-Final on 31 March 1996?

197. What was the score of the 'Derby' game at Maine Road on 6 April 1996?

198. Who were United's opponents at Elm Park in the Fourth Round of the FA Cup?

199. United recorded their first away victory of the 1995-6 season on a Monday night (Sky Sports) live game. Who did they beat?

200. Who chested the ball out to Eric Cantona for him to fire home the only goal of the 1996 FA Cup Final?

ANSWERS ON PAGE 143

27 RED DEVIL: ERIC CANTONA

201. When Eric played football for his French junior school he followed in his father's footsteps by starting off in the same position that his dad used to play. Can you name the position?

202. At which French First Division club did Eric commence his footballing career?

203. Prior to joining Leeds United in 1992 Eric had been on trial with another Premier League side. Name them.

204. 'I am in love with Manchester United. It is like finding a _ _ _ _ who has given me the perfect _ _ _ _ _ _ _ _.' Can you fill in the two missing words from this statement made by Eric about his feelings towards the club?

205. In October 1989, whilst playing for France, Eric scored against a Manchester United goalkeeper. Who was in goal for the opposing nation?

206. Eric has written a number of poems but what is the name of the nineteenth-century Symbolist poet whose work Eric admires?

207. What sports company sponsored Eric during his Old Trafford career?

208. In March 1994 Eric was sent off in two successive games. Who were United's opponents in the two matches?

209. How much did Eric cost United when they purchased him from Leeds?

210. Eric made his United debut against Manchester City in December 1992 when he came on as a substitute. Whom did he replace?

ANSWERS ON PAGE 143

28 PICTURE QUIZ – ROUND 7

1. I joined United in November 1985 and made my United debut that month against Watford (h). Who am I?

2. With which club did I win a First Division Championship medal in 1980-1?

3. What club did I sign for when I left United in December 1990?

4. How much did United pay for me, £275,000, £475,000 or £550,000?

5. How many league goals did I score during the 1987-8 season?

ANSWERS ON PAGE 143

211. Name the team United defeated on the opening day of the league campaign.

212. How many goals did Denis Irwin score in United's FA Cup games?

213. Nicky Butt made an appearance as substitute in his only FA Cup tie of the season. Can you name the opposition?

214. Bryan Robson scored only one league goal all season. Can you name the side he scored against?

215. United's lowest league gate of the season was 41,829. Who were the 'unattractive' visitors?

216. How many league points did the Reds end the season with, 92, 93 or 94?

217. United lost four games in the league. Three of the defeats were against London clubs. Can you name the only other team to have beaten them in the league?

218. How many times did United achieve a league double during the season?

219. Can you name the United substitute who scored in the FA Cup Final?

220. In total, how many games did United play in the FA Cup?

ANSWERS ON PAGE 143

30 THE 1990s IN THE LEAGUE

221. United's first league defeat during the 1993-4 season came on 11 September 1993. Can you name the side that beat them?

222. Can you name the referee who sent off Eric Cantona when United played Crystal Palace at Selhurst Park on 25 January 1995?

223. Which London side beat United 4-1 at Old Trafford on New Year's Day 1992?

224. Only three United players scored more than ten league goals during the 1994-5 season. Name them.

225. Can you name the only Reds player to have scored a Premier League hat-trick in the 1992-3 season?

226. United's first-ever league visit to Swindon's County Ground came in the 1993-4 season, but what was the score?

227. How many points did the Reds finish behind Leeds United in the race for the 1991-2 Championship?

228. What illness caused Lee Sharpe to miss the early part of the 1992-3 season?

229. Can you name the team that Mark Hughes scored his first 1994-5 league goal against?

230. How many points did the Reds secure from their last seven league games of the 1992-3 season?

ANSWERS ON PAGE 143

31 IN THE HOT SEAT – UNITED MANAGERS

231. Dave Sexton's last game in charge of United was a home game on the final day of the 1980-1 season. Who did the Reds beat 1-0 that day?

232. Which ex-United manager once managed the national side of Iran?

233. Can you name the United manager who has spent the shortest period of time in office?

234. Following his dismissal by United which club appointed Tommy Docherty as their manager in the summer of 1977?

235. Who did Alex Ferguson bring with him to Old Trafford as his Assistant Manager, when he became United manager in 1986?

236. Can you name United's manager from 1900-12?

237. How many different managers have been in charge at Old Trafford since the end of the Second World War?

238. Apart from Sir Matt Busby, who is the only other United manager to have been named Manager of the Year?

239. United have only ever had one Player/Manager in their history. Can you name him?

240. Who did Alex Ferguson describe as a 'prat' after hearing his comments on the Reds' FA Cup Fourth Round victory over Norwich City in January 1994?

ANSWERS ON PAGE 143

32
PICTURE QUIZ – ROUND 8

1. Under which two United managers did Jesper Olsen serve at Old Trafford?

2. During his time at United Olsen won only one Winner's medal. Can you name the competition and year?

3. What job did Olsen have prior to becoming a professional footballer?

4. When he left United during the 1988-9 season he moved to a French club. Name it.

5. Can you name the English club side, beginning with the letter 'S', who gave him a trial in March 1992?

ANSWERS ON PAGE 144

33 1994-5 LEAGUE GAMES

241. Who scored United's first league goal of the season?

242. Who scored a late winner for United when they played away at Wimbledon on 7 March 1995?

243. Can you name the United substitute who scored United's second goal of their 2-0 home win over Liverpool?

244. Which team were the first to defeat United in the Premier League?

245. United didn't concede a league goal at Old Trafford until 27 December. Who were the visitors?

246. Keith Gillespie scored his only goal of the season in a league game at Old Trafford in October 1994. Can you name the team he scored against?

247. Andrei Kanchelskis scored a hat-trick against Manchester City in the 'Derby' game at Old Trafford, but who else scored in the 5-0 win?

248. United scored five penalties in their 42 league games. Who scored them?

249. Can you name all the goalscorers in United's 9-0 demolition of Ipswich Town at Old Trafford on 4 March 1995?

250. Who scored United's last league goal of the season?

ANSWERS ON PAGE 144

34 RED DEVIL: GEORGE BEST

251. Did George make his league debut for the Reds in 1961, 1962 or 1963?

252. Can you name the two major football awards he won in 1968?

253. For how many seasons was George United's top goalscorer?

254. How many seasons did George spend at Craven Cottage, Fulham?

255. When George made his debut for Stockport County did he score 2, 3 or 4 times that day?

256. In January 1970 George was suspended following an incident in a game. How many games did his suspension cover?

257. How many goals did he score against Northampton Town in a Fifth Round FA Cup tie in 1970?

258. What name did the Portuguese press give George following United's superb 5-1 European Cup Quarter-Final win over Benfica in Lisbon in 1966?

259. In what year did he make his last appearance for United?

260. What was the name of the US Soccer team that George played for in Los Angeles after he left United?

ANSWERS ON PAGE 144

35 GENERAL – ROUND 3

261. What have ex-United players, Brian Kidd, Denis Law, Sammy McIlroy, Peter Barnes and John Gidman all got in common?

262. United entertained Glasgow Celtic for Bryan Robson's Testimonial. What was the final score?

263. At what age did Wilf McGuinness become the manager of United, 31, 34, or 37?

264. What illness forced Billy Garton to prematurely retire from football in 1991?

265. What role did Archibald Leitch play in the history of Manchester United Football Club?

266. To the nearest 2,000, what was United's average league home attendance during the 1975-6 season?

267. Can you name the former United player who returned to Old Trafford in January 1993, some 18 months after leaving the club?

268. In what year did Nobby Stiles make his first team debut for the Reds?

269. Which sports company sponsors Roy Keane's football boots?

270. United won the FA Cup in 1963 but in what position did they finish in the league?

ANSWERS ON PAGE 144

36 PICTURE QUIZ – ROUND 9

1. Denis is noted for his dislike of England's football team. So, rather than watch the 1966 World Cup Final, Denis spent his time doing something else. What did he do?

2. Against which club did Denis score seven goals, over the two legs, in a 1968-9 European Cup tie?

3. Denis scored against England at Wembley in 1963. Who was he playing for?

4. In what year was Denis voted the European Footballer of the Year?

5. Where was Denis when United beat Benfica to lift the 1968 European Cup?

ANSWERS ON PAGE 144

37 LEAGUE POSITIONS

All you have to do here is match the season with the correct league position in which United finished for each season.

271.	1970-1	4th
272.	1972-3	2nd
273.	1973-4	10th
274.	1975-6	18th
275.	1976-7	9th
276.	1977-8	8th
277.	1978-9	6th
278.	1979-80	11th
279.	1983-4	3rd
280.	1986-7	21st

ANSWERS ON PAGE 144

38 THE 1980s – ROUND 1

281. In the 1980-1 season, did United win, draw or lose the majority of their league games?

282. Name either one of the two players who made their United debut on the opening day of the 1981-2 season.

283. Can you name the on-loan player who made five appearances (two as a sub) for the Reds during the 1982-3 season.

284. United's best win of the 1983-4 season was a 5-0 victory away from home in a game which was shown live on TV. Who did the Reds beat?

285. Who scored United's goal in the 1984 European Cup Winners' Cup Semi-Final second leg against Juventus?

286. In the 1984-5 season, United played the same team on both the opening and final days of the league campaign. Name the team.

287. Who beat United 3 - 2 on the final day of the 1982-3 season, thereby preventing them from finishing as Division 1 Runners-up?

288. Can you name the player who joined United in October 1980 only to be sold back to his former club less than two years later?

289. Who was the Reds' top goalscorer of the 1980-1 season and how many goals did he score?

290. Name three of the four players who wore the No.5 shirt for United in league matches during the 1984-5 season.

ANSWERS ON PAGE 144

39 SENDINGS OFF

291. How many times during his United career was Bobby Charlton sent off?

292. Name the United forward who was sent off at Stamford Bridge on 18 August 1971.

293. For what reason was Andrei Kanchelskis sent off in the 1994 Coca-Cola Cup Final?

294. Which United player was dismissed in the first game of the 1994-5 season?

295. Who were United's opponents when Mark Hughes was sent off in London in November 1994?

296. Can you name the United player who received his marching orders in the away leg of the 1968 World Club Championship game against Estudiantes de la Plata?

297. In the return game with Estudiantes another United player was sent off. Can you name him?

298. What was the name of the referee who sent off Kevin Moran in the 1985 FA Cup Final?

299. How many times was Jim Holton sent off during his first nine games for the Reds, 2, 3 or 4?

300. Can you name the United star who was sent off during the Reds' 1992 UEFA Cup exit at the hands of Torpedo Moscow?

ANSWERS ON PAGE 144

40
PICTURE QUIZ – ROUND 10

1. Eric has played for six French League sides. Name four of them.

2. Against which club did Eric score his last goal for United before his lengthy suspension began in January 1995?

3. Eric scored his first Manchester 'Derby' goal in a 1-1 draw at Maine Road in March 1993. Who crossed the ball for him to head home?

4. How many caps did Eric win with France, 43, 53 or 63?

5. What age was Eric when he retired?

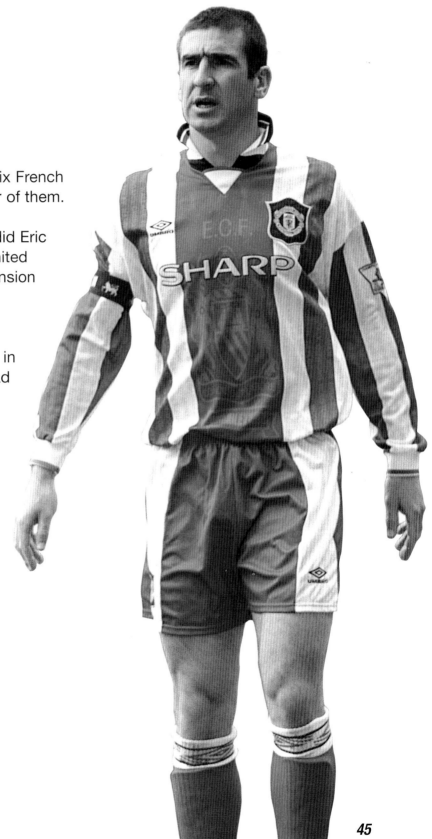

ANSWERS ON PAGE 145

41 GENERAL – ROUND 4

301. Can you name the football sticker company which sponsored United's Family Stand in the late 1980s?

302. When Mickey Thomas left United what club did he join?

303. Who did United play in the 1991 European Super Cup Final?

304. What was Paul Ince's shirt number in the 1990 FA Cup Final and Replay against Crystal Palace?

305. Stuart Pearson and a United team mate both made their England debuts on the same day. Name Stuart's co-debutant.

306. Can you name the former United player who managed Bolton Wanderers between 1974 and 1980?

307. Name the Reds defender who made his debut for the club on the same day that George Best played his last game for United.

308. How many Premier League games did Raimond van der Gouw play during the 1996-7 season?

309. Which team missed three penalties against United in the space of only 8 minutes in February 1980?

310. Name the ex-United player, who when he was a manager, allowed Ralph Milne to join United in 1988.

ANSWERS ON PAGE 145

42 TELEVISION STARS

311. Which former United player has had his voice used in Tango advertisements?

312. Who were United's opponents in December 1983 when the BBC screened their first-ever live Match of the Day?

313. In what year was the first live screening of the Manchester 'Derby', 1986, 1991 or 1996?

314. United won 5-0 in a game which was screened live in February 1984. Can you recall their opponents?

315. Can you name the former United goalkeeper who competed in the Gladiators 1994 Christmas Celebrity Special?

316. A former Old Trafford hero was presented with the famous large red book on *This Is Your Life* in November 1991. Name him.

317. Who did United beat 1-0 in a live televised game on 21 December 1997?

318. Were the Reds first screened in colour on *Match of the Day* in 1969, 1972 or 1975?

319. What was the name of the Breakfast TV station that George Best worked on during the 1980s?

320. United made their first-ever appearance on Sky TV in August 1992. Who did they play and what was the score of the game?

ANSWERS ON PAGE 145

43 FORMER HEROES – ROUND 1

321. A player from the 1968 European Cup winning side managed Japanese club, Mazda, in 1989. Name him.

322. Which member of the 1977 FA Cup winning side played Rugby Union with Sale during the early 1980s?

323. Against which Midlands club did Gary Walsh make his league debut for United?

324. United purchased Paul Parker from Queens Park Rangers but which team did Paul play for before he moved to Loftus Road?

325. Who was United's goalkeeper in the 1990 FA Charity Shield?

326. Who holds the record for the most league appearances for United?

327. Only two survivors of the Munich Air Disaster played in United's first match after the tragedy. Can you name them?

328. Can you name the United star who adorned billboards, advertising Heineken lager with his toothless grin?

329. At which league club did Dion Dublin begin his professional career?

330. Who was the first-ever black player to play for the Reds?

ANSWERS ON PAGE 145

44 PICTURE QUIZ – ROUND 11

1. At which league club did Steve begin his career?

2. In the 1990-1 season Steve was United's joint top goalscorer in the league. How many league goals did he score?

3. When United met Everton in the 1995 FA Cup Final, Steve's defensive partner at Carrow Road lined up against him. Can you name him?

4. Name one of the two unfortunate things which happened to Steve when he made his United debut against Portsmouth.

5. What Winner's medal did Steve win in 1985?

ANSWERS ON PAGE 145

45 THE 1970s – ROUND 2

331. Can you name the famous Scottish manager who it is said was asked to be United's manager in April 1971?

332. United lost only one game at Old Trafford during the 1975-6 season. Who beat them?

333. United won the Second Division Championship in 1974-5. Who was the club's leading goalscorer that season?

334. Which Yorkshire club did the Reds draw 4-4 with on 7 December 1974?

335. Which United manager signed Martin Buchan from Aberdeen in March 1972?

336. On which club's ground did United win the first-ever penalty shoot-out, in English football, during a Watney Cup match in August 1970?

337. How many times did United draw 0-0 at Old Trafford during the 1975-6 league season, 0, 2 or 12?

338. By how many points did the Reds win the 1974-5 Second Division Championship?

339. What season during the 1970s did Manchester City finish ten points clear of the Reds?

340. When United were relegated at the end of season 1973-4 how many points had they accumulated?

ANSWERS ON PAGE 145

46 LEAGUE CUP – ROUND 2

341. Which club put the Reds out of the 1994-5 competition?

342. Where, in London, did United win 6-2 in the Fourth Round during the 1990-91 season?

343. Who scored Liverpool's winner against United in the 1983 Final?

344. Who did United meet in the 1992 Semi-Final?

345. Who scored United's extra-time winner in that Semi-Final?

346. Which former United goalkeeper was in goal for the opposition in the 1992 Semi-Final?

347. How many First Division sides (there was no Premier League) did the Reds meet in the 1990-91 competition?

348. In what season did United first participate in the League Cup, 1957-8, 1960-1 or 1970-1?

349. Can you name the club that defeated the Reds in both the 1983-4 and 1987-8 competitions?

350. What colour of kit did the Reds play in when they won the 1992 Final?

ANSWERS ON PAGE 145

47 THE GREY KIT 1995-6

351. What colour of away kit did the grey one replace?

352. United wore their new grey kit on the opening day of the 1995-6 season. Who provided the opposition?

353. What was the score of the above game?

354. How many times did United wear the kit in a competitive match?

355. How many league points did United win in the kit?

356. Against which club did United secure their first point(s) in the grey kit?

357. Can you name the only three players to have scored a league goal whilst wearing the grey kit?

358. What sponsorship logo adorned the front of the grey shirt?

359. What colour of kit replaced the grey one?

360. What was the reason given by Manchester United when they decided to discard the kit?

ANSWERS ON PAGE 145

48 PICTURE QUIZ – ROUND 12

1. Who is this United star of the 1970s?

2. Which London club did he make his United debut against in the capital?

3. Six months after leaving Old Trafford he became reunited with one of his former managers. Can you name the manager and club concerned?

4. How many international caps did he win with the Republic of Ireland, 36, 46 or 56?

5. From which Irish club side did United purchase him for £20,000?

ANSWERS ON PAGE 145

49 MANCHESTER 'DERBY' GAMES

361. Can you name the United player who scored two penalties in the 2-2 draw at Old Trafford on 15 March 1978?

362. Who scored the only goal of the game in the hundredth 'Derby' match at Old Trafford on 22 March 1980?

363. United drew 1-1 with City at Maine Road on 20 March 1993 in a Premier League fixture. City took the lead but who equalised for the Reds?

364. Can you name the United player who made his league debut against City at Maine Road on 13 March 1974?

365. What was the special about the 0-0 'Derby' match at Maine Road on 20 September 1947?

366. Prior to United's 5-0 demolition of City in November 1994 in what year did they last put five past their neighbours?

367. United first met City in a Premier League 'Derby' game in December 1992. What was the score?

368. Can you name the only United boss never to have lost a 'Derby' game?

369. What was the score of the 110th 'Derby' which was staged at Old Trafford on 7 March 1987, 1-0, 2-0, or 3-0?

370. In May 1976 the son of United's manager, at that time, played for City in a 'Derby' game. Name the father and son involved.

ANSWERS ON PAGE 146

50 ERIC THE KING

371. What was the shirt number worn by Eric in both games against Galatasaray in the 1993-4 European Cup?

372. In what year did Eric win the PFA Player of The Year Award?

373. Eric has a tattoo on his chest. What is it of?

374. How many first team appearances did Eric make for United, 180, 197 or 204?

375. How many FA Charity Shields did Eric win?

376. What season was his most productive for United in terms of goals scored?

377. What Award did Eric win in 1996?

378. How many league and cup goals did Eric score for United in competitive matches?

379. How many games did Eric start as a substitute for United?

380. What percentage of games did United lose when Eric was on the pitch?

ANSWERS ON PAGE 146

51 RED DEVIL: PETER SCHMEICHEL

381. True or False – Schmeichel played for United in the 1994 Coca-Cola Cup Final?

382. Against which club did Schmeichel score and thereby save United's then unbeaten run at Old Trafford in European competition?

383. Can you name the Turkish side who were said to be interested in signing Schmeichel in 1995?

384. During the 1994-5 season how many goals did Schmeichel concede at Old Trafford in Premiership games?

385. Against which club did Schmeichel make his United debut?

386. Since joining United Schmeichel has only ever played one full season without missing a league game. Name the season.

387. Where in Denmark was Schmeichel born, Copenhagen, Gladsaxe or Brondby?

388. How many Coca-Cola Cup ties did Peter Schmeichel play during the 1995-6 season?

389. Who made his league debut for United when he replaced Schmeichel in goal during a game against Crystal Palace on 19 November 1994?

390. What are the two things that Schmeichel kicks prior to the referee blowing his whistle to start the game?

ANSWERS ON PAGE 146

56

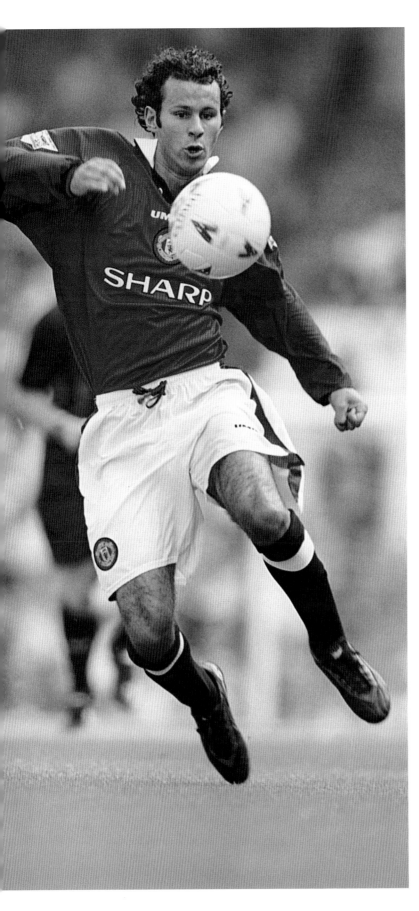

52
PICTURE QUIZ – ROUND 13

1. Against which team did Ryan make his league debut for United?

2. In what competition did Ryan win his first medal with United?

3. What footballing record did he set in 1993?

4. Which Italian side was reputedly interested in signing him for £10 million in 1993?

5. What is his middle name, Joseph, John or Thomas?

ANSWERS ON PAGE 146

53 SIR MATT BUSBY

391. As a player Matt Busby won a Winner's medal in 1934. Can you name the competition in which he played?

392. Can you name the first professional football club for which he played?

393. Can you name the player that Matt Busby signed from Glasgow Celtic in February 1946?

394. What was the first trophy Matt Busby won as manager of Manchester United?

395. How many First Division Championships did United win under Matt Busby, 5, 6 or 7?

396. How many times did Matt Busby lead United to the FA Cup Final and how many of those times did they win the cup?

397. True or False – United finished Division One Runners-Up six times under Matt Busby?

398. In what year was Matt Busby appointed the manager of Manchester United?

399. How many times did United win the FA Charity Shield outright under Matt Busby during the 1960s?

400. What honour did he receive in London in 1968?

ANSWERS ON PAGE 146

401. In what year did Steve Coppell win his first full England cap?

402. Can you recall the year that Peter Beardsley played for United?

403. In what year did United goalkeeper, Chris Turner, leave United to join Sheffield Wednesday?

404. In what year did Arnold Muhren join United?

405. Name either of the two years that Mark Hughes won the PFA Player of the Year Award.

406. Can you remember the year United launched their own lager called 'Red Devil'?

407. Can you name the year Wyn Davies left Manchester City and joined United?

408. Paddy Crerand scored only one goal in European competition for United. It came against Benfica. Name the year.

409. During which decade this century were United relegated to Division 2 twice?

410. In what year did Eric Cantona sign for United?

ANSWERS ON PAGE 146

55 GENERAL – ROUND 5

411. During the 1985-6 season what shirt number did Norman Whiteside wear?

412. In the 1973-4 season Old Trafford only had one league crowd exceeding 60,000. Who were the opposition that day?

413. Can you name the United centre-forward who replaced Nat Lofthouse in the England team in 1956?

414. United beat Nottingham Forest in the Quarter-Final of the 1983 Milk Cup. What was the score of the game?

415. Who did the Reds defeat 2-1 on the final day of the inaugural Premier League season?

416. Who were United's opponents in the 1983 FA Cup Final and by what means of transport did they arrive at Wembley?

417. Two Scots made their United debuts on 20 January 1973 against West Ham United. Name either of them.

418. Can you name the Glasgow Celtic player who Ron Atkinson attempted to sign in 1983?

419. Who wore the No.7 shirt for the Reds in the 1992 Rumbelows League Cup Final?

420. Name the oldest player of the 1968 European Cup Winning team.

ANSWERS ON PAGE 146

56 PICTURE QUIZ – ROUND 14

1. He signed for United in September 1981. Can you name him?

2. How many FA Cup Finals did he appear in for United?

3. From which club did United purchase him?

4. How much did he cost United, £500,000, £600,000 or £700,000?

5. Against which Welsh side did he make his United debut?

ANSWERS ON PAGE 147

57 INTERNATIONAL MIXED BAG – ROUND 2

421. In which city was Ryan Giggs born?

422. Which team did Matt Busby manage in 1948 beating Holland 4-3 at Highbury and France 1-0 at Craven Cottage?

423. How many full England caps did David Pegg win before his death in the Munich Air Disaster?

424. Name the two United players who appeared in the 1994 World Cup Finals in the USA.

425. Which Irish former United player formed his own fan club in 1987?

426. Brian McClair won his first full Scotland cap after he moved to Manchester United. True or False?

427. How many full England caps did United goalkeeper Jack Crompton win?

428. Gary Bailey won his first full England cap in 1985 in a friendly game. Name the opposition.

429. A Manchester United player was voted 'Best England Player' in the 1980 European Championships in Italy. Name the player.

430. In what year did Mike Duxbury win his first full England cap, 1981, 1982 or 1983?

ANSWERS ON PAGE 147

58 EUROPEAN CUP – ROUND 2

431. Can you name the Irish side which United met in the First Round of the 1968-9 European Cup?

432. Manchester United played their first-ever European Cup tie on 12 September 1956. Name the city they played in.

433. When United met Borussia Dortmund in the First Round of the 1956-7 competition, what was the aggregate score over both legs?

434. Who was the next player up the Wembley steps after Bobby Charlton following United's success over Benfica in the 1968 Final?

435. Name United's opponents in the First Round of the 1965-6 competition.

436. When United met Red Star Belgrade in the second leg of their Quarter-Final tie on 5 February 1958, what was the score in Belgrade?

437. Who were the two captains when United and Benfica contested the 1968 Final?

438. United were defeated in the 1966 Semi-Final. Who beat them?

439. In the 1967-8 competition United played Hibernians Valetta. Which country do they come from?

440. Who scored Manchester United's first-ever goal in a European Cup fixture?

ANSWERS ON PAGE 147

59 FA CUP – ROUND 2

441. At which ground did United and Oldham Athletic play their 1994 FA Cup Semi-Final replay?

442. Name the Lancashire side United defeated 3-0 in the Fourth Round of the 1970 FA Cup.

443. Who scored the most FA Cup goals for United, George Best or Bobby Charlton?

444. Who replaced the injured Ray Wood in United's goal during the 1957 FA Cup Final?

445. Which United player was the first post-war player to captain a Scottish and English FA Cup winning side?

446. Arthur Albiston won three FA Cup Winner's medals during his United career. Name the years.

447. Can you name the United goalkeeper who won an FA Cup Winner's medal in the 1963 Final?

448. How many FA Cup Winner's medals did Gordon Strachan win with United?

449. In the Sixth Round of the 1958 FA Cup United played a team from the Midlands. Name their opponents.

450. United visited Wales for an FA Cup Fourth Round tie on 26 January 1957. Name the side they defeated 5-0.

ANSWERS ON PAGE 147

60 PICTURE QUIZ – ROUND 15

1. Bobby won only one FA Cup Winner's medal during his career. What shirt number did he wear in the Final of 1963?

2. How many full international caps did he win for England, 101, 103 or 106?

3. What club did he become player/manager of when he left United?

4. In what year did he win both the Player of the Year Award and the European Player of the Year Award?

5. In what year did Bobby make his international debut for England?

ANSWERS ON PAGE 147

61 UNITED IN EUROPE – ROUND 2

451. What was the score of the game when United met Juventus at Old Trafford in the 1983-4 European Cup Winners' Cup Semi-Final?

452. Name the Hungarian side United played in the First Round of the UEFA Cup in the 1984-5 season.

453. In the 1964-5 Inter Cities Fairs Cup, United met a club named Djurgardens IF. Which country did they come from?

454. How many defeats did United suffer in the 1996-7 UEFA Champions League?

455. Name one of the players who scored for United against Dundee United in their 3-2 UEFA Cup, Third Round, second leg encounter in December 1984.

456. Which Portuguese side knocked United out of the European Cup Winners' Cup of 1977-8?

457. Can you name the Spanish side that United defeated in the Quarter-Final of the European Cup in the 1956-7 season?

458. In the 1968-9 European Cup, United played a team that they also met in the 1996-7 competition. Name the team.

459. United were knocked out of the 1980-1 UEFA Cup in the First Round by Polish side, Widzew Lodz. What was the aggregate score over the two legs?

460. Name the three teams that made up United's Group in the 1996-7 UEFA Champions League.

ANSWERS ON PAGE 147

62 FORMER HEROES – ROUND 2

461. Can you name the former United player who captained Stoke City during the mid 1980s?

462. Who was the first-ever £100,000-plus Manchester United player?

463. Who scored United's only goal in the 1994 Coca-Cola Cup Final?

464. A former United star of the late 1970s and early 1980s became the manager of Airdrie in the summer of 1987. Name him.

465. Can you name United's goalkeeper when they won the First Division Championship in 1964-5?

466. Only one United player appeared in all 60 of their league and cup games during the 1982-3 season. Who was he?

467. Which former United captain wrote the song 'Old Trafford Blues'?

468. During the 1960s two United players were called 'Nobby'. Nobby Stiles was one of them. Name the other.

469. Who was the United goalkeeper who, despite making 247 appearances for the club, never won an honour with them?

470. When United played Liverpool in March 1985, five United players made their Anfield debut. Name three of them.

ANSWERS ON PAGE 147

63 FRIENDLIES AND TESTIMONIALS

471. United played Preston North End at Deepdale in April 1978 in a Testimonial Match for a member of the 1968 European Cup Winning team. Can you name him?

472. Norman Whiteside received a Testimonial Match at the end of the 1991-2 season. Who were United's opponents?

473. United defeated Glasgow Celtic and AS Bari whilst touring Canada in May 1970 and won a cup named after a Canadian city. Can you name the city?

474. On 29 July 1992 United played a Champions of Europe Commemoration Match. Name the former European Cup Winners they played.

475. United played SL Benfica in Portugal on 1 December 1992. Can you name the player whose Testimonial it was?

476. On 17 May 1993 United drew 4-4 with Arsenal in a farewell match for a former Highbury star. Name the player concerned.

477. Between July 1992 and August 1992 United toured Scandinavia playing games in two different countries. Which Scandinavian countries did they visit?

478. Why was Arthur Albiston's Testimonial Match against Glasgow Celtic called off in May 1987?

479. Who were United's opposition for Martin Buchan's Testimonial Match?

480. In 1978 United played a friendly at Old Trafford to celebrate their Centenary Year. Which famous European club did they play?

ANSWERS ON PAGE 147

64
PICTURE QUIZ – ROUND 16

1. What club did Sparky join on loan in November 1987?

2. In what competition did he make his United debut?

3. On his full international debut Sparky scored the winning goal. Who did Wales defeat?

4. In his first full season for the Reds he was United's top goalscorer. Name the season.

5. Against which country did he score a spectacular scissors kick goal in a World Cup qualifying game at Wrexham in 1985?

ANSWERS ON PAGE 148

65 CHAMPIONS 1996-7 – ROUND 2

481. Who did United play at Old Trafford on New Year's Day?

482. Of United's last four league games, how many ended in score draws?

483. When United met Leeds United at Old Trafford in December the game was decided by a Cantona penalty. Name the Leeds player who gave the penalty away.

484. Can you name the Premiership manager who said after his team beat the Reds in March that 'We will stay up and United will win the title'?

485. When United won 2-1 at Old Trafford in January they went to the top of the league for the first time since September. Who did they beat?

486. Name the first team to defeat United in the Premiership during the season.

487. When United and Middlesbrough drew 3-3 at Old Trafford towards the end of the season, who were the scorers for the Reds?

488. During the season, with which team did United draw both their Premiership games 0-0?

489. Over the two league games between them, against which side did the Reds score the most goals?

490. How many points did United finish the season with, 73, 74 or 75?

ANSWERS ON PAGE 148

66 IRISH CONNECTION

491. Roy Keane scored twice on his European debut for United. Who were the Reds' opponents?

492. When Northern Ireland played Holland in 1976 how many United players were capped in the game?

493. A former United player later became a First Team coach at Glasgow Celtic. Was it Mick Martin, Gerry Daly or Ashley Grimes?

494. Sammy McIlroy was United's top goalscorer in the league during the 1973-4 season. How many goals did he score?

495. Can you name the Irishman who captained United to FA Cup glory in 1963?

496. In September 1990 a United player, who had been a regular in the Northern Ireland side, was dropped by his country for the first time in eight years. Can you name him?

497. Which player has won the most caps for Northern Ireland whilst playing for United?

498. David McCreery and Chris McGrath both played for the same US club during the mid-1970s. What was the name of the club?

499. Who did Wilf McGuinness once describe as 'an Irish Bobby Charlton'?

500. Can you name the Irish midfield player who appeared in five FA Cup Finals at Wembley between 1963 and 1973?

ANSWERS ON PAGE 148

67 DOUBLE DOUBLE WINNERS – ROUND 2

501. How many Premier League games did the Reds lose during the 1995-6 season?

502. Who scored United's winner against Sunderland at Roker Park in the FA Cup Third Round Replay?

503. When United beat Newcastle United at Old Trafford on 27 December 1995, what was the score of the game and who scored for the Reds?

504. How many FA Cup games did United play on their way to lifting the trophy, including the Final?

505. Roy Keane was sent off in a Premiership fixture at Old Trafford on 28 October 1995. Who were the opponents that day?

506. United met a Lancashire side in the FA Cup Fifth Round. Name them.

507. Who were the Reds' opponents when Eric returned from his nine-month ban on 1 October 1995?

508. Can you name the side United defeated in the Sixth Round of the FA Cup?

509. United suffered two successive away defeats during December 1995. Name the two teams to beat them.

510. How many times did United score in the 90th minute in FA Cup games during the 1995-6 season?

ANSWERS ON PAGE 148

68 PICTURE QUIZ – ROUND 17

1. David made his United league debut on 2 April 1995. Name the opposition.

2. On the opening day of the 1996-7 season David scored against Wimbledon from his own half. What distance was his shot officially measured at?

3. In January 1997 David scored two brilliant goals against the same opposition in consecutive weeks. What team were on the receiving end?

4. David made his international debut in a World Cup qualifying game in September 1996. Who were England's opponents?

5. In the 1996-7 Champions League David scored in consecutive games. Name the two clubs he netted against.

ANSWERS ON PAGE 148

69
RED DEVIL: GARY PALLISTER

511. Gary was part of Terry Venables' first-ever England team, true or false?

512. What award did he win in 1992?

513. Where in England was Gary born?

514. Gary scored his first-ever European goal for the Reds in the European Cup Winners' Cup. Who were United's opponents?

515. He made his international debut for England against Hungary in Budapest. Can you name the year?

516. Pally scored two Premiership goals during the 1994-5 season. Name either of the two clubs he netted against.

517. Up to the end of the 1996-7 season, how many goals had Gary scored for England?

518. How much did United pay Middlesbrough for his services?

519. How many goals did he score in United's 3-1 win at Anfield on 19 April 1997?

520. True or False – both David May and Ronny Johnsen made more First Team appearances for the Reds than Pally during the 1996-7 season?

ANSWERS ON PAGE 148

70 UP FRONT

521. Dion Dublin signed for United in 1992. Which club did he leave to join the Reds?

522. Can you name the United forward who scored for his country during the 1978 World Cup Finals in Argentina?

523. What was Stuart Pearson's nickname at Old Trafford?

524. Paul Scholes scored twice on his United debut in a Coca-Cola Cup tie. Name the team on the receiving end.

525. I made six appearances and one as substitute for United during a loan spell in season 1983-4. Who am I?

526. Can you name the Ipswich Town goalkeeper who had five goals put past him by Andy Cole during a Premiership game in March 1995?

527. What shirt number was usually worn by Lou Macari during his career with United?

528. How many Scottish league clubs did Denis Law play for?

529. Can you name the country George Best scored a hat-trick against in a European Championship game in April 1971?

530. Name the United forward who left Old Trafford for Ayresome Park in October 1988.

ANSWERS ON PAGE 148

71 FLOWERS OF SCOTLAND

531. During the 1986 World Cup Finals in Mexico a United player scored his country's only goal of the tournament. Name the player.

532. When Graeme Hogg left the Reds in 1988, which south coast club did he join?

533. Against which England goalkeeper did Denis Law score his only FA Cup Final goal in the 1963 Final?

534. Can you name the United striker who hit five goals in six FA Cup games during the 1958 competition?

535. Name the Reds' midfield player who was sent off for fighting in European games against Ferencvaros and Partizan Belgrade during the 1960s.

536. What was Matt Busby's occupation prior to becoming a footballer?

537. Where in Scotland was Brian McClair born?

538. Name the goalkeeper who was dropped by Alex Ferguson for the 1990 FA Cup Final Replay.

539. Who was United's manager when they won the 1935-6 Second Division Championship?

540. A United winger was in the Scotland squad at the 1974 World Cup Finals in West Germany. Name him.

ANSWERS ON PAGE 148

72 PICTURE QUIZ – ROUND 18

1. From which Irish club did United purchase Paul for £30,000 in April 1982?

2. How many FA Cup Winner's medals did he win during his career at Old Trafford?

3. What medal did Paul win in 1994?

4. In what year did he move to Aston Villa from United?

5. In what year did he win his first of many international caps for the Republic of Ireland?

ANSWERS ON PAGE 149

73 INTERNATIONAL DEBUTS

Rearrange the countries so that they correspond with the player who made his international debut against them.

541.	Nicky Butt	Luxembourg
542.	Eric Cantona	Belgium
543.	Andy Cole	Japan
544.	Ryan Giggs	Chile
545.	Denis Irwin	Mexico
546.	Roy Keane	China
547.	Gary Neville	Jamaica
548.	Ole Gunnar Solskjaer	Uruguay
549.	Brian McClair	Morocco
550.	Phil Neville	West Germany

ANSWERS ON PAGE 149

74 FOREIGN AFFAIRS

All you have to do here is identify the player from the clues given.

551. I cost United £1.5 million. During the Championship winning season, 1996-7, I scored three league goals.

552. I was born on 18 November 1963 and signed for United on 6 August 1991. My league debut for the Reds was against Notts County.

553. In my first season with the Reds I collected an FA Cup Winner's medal. During the 1980s I made 92 appearances for United and scored 18 goals.

554. My previous clubs include Molde and FK Clausenengen. In my first ten games for my country I scored five times.

555. I joined United in 1992. My league debut for the Reds came in a Manchester 'Derby' game.

556. I joined United from Ajax Amsterdam and made 148 appearances for the Reds. I was signed by Ron Atkinson for £800,000.

557. I was born on 23 January 1969. I signed for United in May 1991 and in my first full season at Old Trafford I made 28 appearances and scored five goals.

558. I am a Norwegian international and joined United in the summer of 1996. One of my former clubs was Besiktas of Turkey.

559. Dave Sexton signed me in 1979. Things didn't really work out for me and I left Old Trafford after making only 25 appearances for the club.

560. I made my United league debut against Everton at Old Trafford on 21 August 1996 but started my professional career at SK Sporting.

ANSWERS ON PAGE 149

75 THE 1980s – ROUND 2

561. Name the United defender who scored an own-goal against Liverpool in the 1985 FA Cup Semi-Final replay at Maine Road.

562. Who scored United's two goals in the above game?

563. Who published a book entitled *United To Win* in 1984?

564. Can you name the ex-Everton player whose football career seemed finished when he quit the game with a bad back injury only for United to give him a second chance by repaying his insurance money to take him back into the Football League?

565. In February 1986 the Reds purchased their second Danish player. Name him.

566. When United finished fourth in Division 1 in 1985-6, how many consecutive times had they finished in the same position?

567. About which United manager was Martin Edwards speaking when he said, 'I am sure that we have made a wise choice. We had to move quickly, once we decided to get rid of X-we wanted to replace him as quickly as possible'?

568. Who was Jesper Olsen speaking about when he said, 'There is no doubt about it, X hit me – it was no accident'?

569. Which club did Ron Atkinson leave to take up his appointment as manager of Manchester United?

570. When Dave Sexton's contract at Old Trafford was terminated in 1981, the contract of his assistant was also terminated. Name his assistant.

ANSWERS ON PAGE 149

1. Against which Lancashire club did Pat make his United debut on 23 February 1963?

2. How much did Matt Busby pay Glasgow Celtic for the young Scot's services?

3. Where in Scotland was Paddy born?

4. Can you name the club he became manager of in 1976?

5. How many Championship medals did he win in his days at Old Trafford?

ANSWERS ON PAGE 149

77 YOUNG GUNS

571. During the 1996-7 season four players whose surname begins with the letter 'C' made First Team appearances for the Reds. Name them.

572. Against which Lancashire club did Terry Cooke make his United league debut on 16 September 1995?

573. From which Yorkshire club did United sign Graeme Tomlinson?

574. When United met Juventus at Old Trafford in the Champions League on 20 November 1996, the game was settled by a penalty. Who conceded the spot kick and who converted it?

575. Name the United player who scored on his league debut for the club on 25 August 1996.

576. About which United player was Alan Shearer speaking when he said, 'You don't realise how good X is until you play with him. He can do so much with a football. He has the world at his feet.'?

577. Can you name the London club against whom Ben Thornley made his United debut on 26 February 1994?

578. Name the player who scored twice for the Reds in their 3-1 Premiership win over Leicester City at Old Trafford on 30 November 1996.

579. Which on-loan United player scored a promotion-clinching goal for Wigan Athletic in April 1997, thereby securing a place for them in Division 2?

580. A player whose surname begins with the letter 'A', turned professional at Old Trafford on 1 July 1994. Name the player.

ANSWERS ON PAGE 149

78 UNITED v LIVERPOOL

581. What was the score between the two teams when they met in the league in April 1988?

582. Which United player was sent off in the above game?

583. From which Cup competition during the 1990-1 season did United eliminate Liverpool?

584. Who were United's scorers in the above match?

585. Who scored for Liverpool in United's 3-1 win at Anfield on 19 April 1997?

586. United drew 3-3 with Liverpool in a pulsating FA Premier League game in January 1994. Can you name the United goalscorers?

587. How many times during the 1980s, excluding replays, did the two sides meet in the FA Cup?

588. Three Scots scored for United when they crushed Liverpool 4-1 at Anfield in December 1969. Can you name them?

589. Liverpool beat United 2-1 at Old Trafford in March 1990. Which Liverpool player scored an own-goal that day?

590. Who scored the only goal of the game when the two sides met in the 1979 FA Cup Semi-Final Replay?

ANSWERS ON PAGE 149

79 NICKNAMES

The following United players all had a nickname during their spell at Old Trafford. Rearrange the nicknames so that they correspond correctly with the name of the player.

591.	Nobby Stiles	'Gunner'
592.	Arthur Albiston	'Happy'
593.	Mark Hughes	'The King'
594.	Jack Rowley	'El Beatle'
595.	Lou Macari	'Merlin'
596.	Denis Law	'The Black Pearl Of Inchicore'
597.	Gordon Hill	'The Black Prince'
598.	Paul McGrath	'Sparky'
599.	Alex Dawson	'Chips'
600.	George Best	'The Judge'

ANSWERS ON PAGE 149

80

PICTURE QUIZ – ROUND 20

1. Name any one of the three North American soccer teams which Brian played for between 1980-81.

2. Who did he replace as Assistant Manager at United in August 1991?

3. Can you name the Lancashire team which Brian briefly managed from January-March 1986?

4. Can you name the club he joined for £110,000 in 1974?

5. Brian celebrated his birthday when United played Benfica at Wembley in the 1968 European Cup Final. How old was he?

ANSWERS ON PAGE 149

81 RED DEVIL: BRIAN McCLAIR

601. In what year did Brian sign for United?

602. How many league appearances did he make during the 1992-3 campaign?

603. In what Cup, during the 1994-5 season, did he captain the Reds?

604. In what year did he make his international debut and who was Scotland's manager at that time?

605. Brian scored his first hat-trick for United in a 4-1 win in April 1988. Can you name the opposition?

606. True or False – Brian scored United's third goal in the 1994 FA Cup Final?

607. How many goals did he score in United's successful 1989-90 FA Cup run, 3, 4 or 5 ?

608. For which Scottish league club did he play part-time while attending Glasgow University?

609. In what year did he score his first full-international goal?

610. During his first season at Old Trafford, Brian became the first United player for more than twenty years to score 20 league goals in a season. Who was the last United player before him to achieve a similar feat?

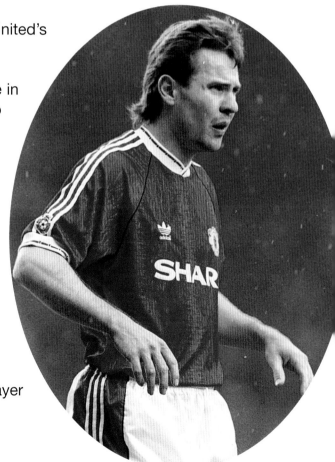

ANSWERS ON PAGE 150

82 TRANSFERS – ROUND 2

611. Name the team that Ray Wilkins joined after leaving United in May 1984.

612. For which club side did Arnold Muhren sign when he left United at the end of the 1984-5 season?

613. Name the Third Division striker signed by Frank O'Farrell for £200,000 in 1972.

614. Can you name the Italian side, beginning with the letter 'B', for which Carlo Sartori signed in 1971?

615. When Paddy Roche left United did he sign for Bury, Brentford or Bolton?

616. Name the Leeds United player who signed for United in the summer of 1983 for £45,000.

617. Who was the manager of Leeds United who allowed Denis Irwin to leave the club on a free transfer in 1986?

618. From which club did United sign Wyn Davies?

619. Which club did Steve Bruce join when he left Old Trafford in 1996?

620. Name the Midlands club that Ashley Grimes joined after leaving Old Trafford.

ANSWERS ON PAGE 150

83 WELSH DRAGONS

621. Can you name the Welsh international player who played for both Manchester clubs during the 1970s?

622. Before joining Barcelona, Mark Hughes made his last international appearance as a United player, against a South American country. Which one?

623. A Manchester United official led Wales to the 1958 World Cup Finals in Sweden. Name the official.

624. How many United players were included in the Welsh squad at the 1990 World Cup Finals in Italy?

625. Name the Welsh international purchased by United from Wrexham in November 1978.

626. Where in Wales was Clayton Blackmore born?

627. He played for United in the 1983 FA Cup Final and made his debut for Wales against Northern Ireland in Belfast shortly after his Wembley appearance. Name him.

628. One of Ryan Giggs' goals was used on the opening titles to *Match of the Day* during the 1993-4 season. Can you name the team he scored against?

629. Who was United's first post-Second World War Welsh international?

630. Name the United player who scored for Wales in their 4-1 win over England at Wrexham in May 1980.

ANSWERS ON PAGE 150

1. Where in Ireland was Denis born?

2. In what year did Denis join the Reds?

3. How many goals did Denis score during the 1996-7 season?

4. Who at United described Denis as 'One of those full-backs you think has been playing so long he must be 60'?

5. Can you name the manager who signed Denis when he left Leeds United?

ANSWERS ON PAGE 150

85 SILVERWARE

631. United won the first five FA Youth Cups. Name the years.

632. Bobby Charlton made his last appearance for United against Verona on 2 May 1973. What was the competition concerned?

633. In what cup competition did Derby County beat the Reds 4-1 in the 1970 Final?

634. Who beat United in the 1985 FA Charity Shield?

635. United met Estudiantes in the 1968 World Club Championship. What South American country do Estudiantes come from?

636. Can you name the competition in which Everton beat the Reds 4-2 at Old Trafford during the 1985-6 season?

637. How many times have United played in the World Club Championship?

638. A former United player played for Southampton against the Reds in the 1976 FA Cup Final. Name him.

639. Name the club's Youth Team that Manchester United's Youth Team defeated in the Final of the 1995 FA Youth Cup.

640. Who captained the Reds in the 1983 Milk Cup Final?

ANSWERS ON PAGE 150

86 GENERAL – ROUND 6

641. Who provided the opposition for Bill Foulkes' Testimonial game in November 1970?

642. Can you name the United goalkeeper of the 1980s whose father played professional football for Ipswich Town?

643. Nobby Stiles wore the No.6 shirt for United in the 1963 FA Cup Final. True or False?

644. Lou Macari paid £140 in a 1981 auction for a pair of football boots which belonged to an ex-United player. Name the player.

645. In what year did Manchester United become a public limited company?

646. What colour of shorts did the Reds start wearing at away games in the 1975-6 season?

647. Can you name the Scottish side that Alex Forsyth joined after leaving Old Trafford?

648. Can you name the last team to have beaten United in an FA Cup Semi-Final?

649. What nickname was given to David McCreery during his time with United?

650. Which United player was booed every time he touched the ball when the Reds played PSV Eindhoven in Round Two of the 1984-5 UEFA Cup?

ANSWERS ON PAGE 150

651. Can you name the former Red with the middle names Johannus Hyacinthus?

652. In what country was Andrei Kanchelskis born?

653. Who was the Swedish international defender that Alex Ferguson attempted to sign in the summer of 1987?

654. A striker who played in the Premiership in the 1992-3 season scored a World Cup goal against Peter Schmeichel in April 1993. Name the player and his country.

655. United had three players in the 1966 England World Cup squad. Name them.

656. The Reds finished third in *World Soccer* magazine's poll for the best team in the world in 1994. Name either of the two sides that finished above them.

657. David Herd won five Scotland caps. How many of them did he win during his Old Trafford career?

658. Name the United player whose former clubs include Go Ahead Eagles and Vitesse Arnhem.

659. Can you name United's two foreigners who appear on the front cover of the book, *Manchester United, The Official Review 96/97,* holding the Premiership Trophy aloft?

660. Who signed for United on the Old Trafford pitch prior to a league game against Wolverhampton Wanderers on 3 October 1981?

ANSWERS ON PAGE 150

88

PICTURE QUIZ – ROUND 22

1. From which club did United sign David?

2. He made his United league debut at Old Trafford on 20 August 1994. Name the Reds' London opponents that day.

3. Where in Lancashire was David born and what team did he support as a young boy?

4. David scored only one goal in the 1996-7 UEFA Champions League campaign. Who did he score against and what was the score of the game?

5. In 1997 Glenn Hoddle called David into the full England squad for the first time. Who was England due to play?

ANSWERS ON PAGE 150

89 RED DEVIL: MARK HUGHES

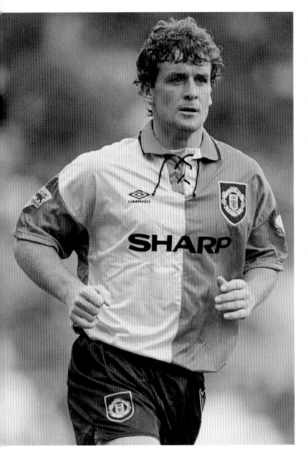

661. When Mark rejoined United after his brief spell at Barcelona, how much did he cost the Reds?

662. Where in Wales was he born?

663. Against which London club did Mark score his last competitive goal for United?

664. In the 1993-4 season Sparky scored a goal that was commemorated in a painting entitled 'The Goal That Inspired The Double'. To what goal does it refer?

665. True or False – Mark scored United's fourth goal in the 1994 FA Cup Final against Chelsea?

666. Can you name the club Sparky scored against on 15 January 1995 in the Premiership and then was immediately substituted?

667. In his early days at United Mark did not play as a centre-forward. Name the position he played in before being switched to lead the attack.

668. How many goals has he scored in FA Cup Finals?

669. Can you name the England international player who played in the same Barcelona side as Mark?

670. Who were United's opponents when he played his last competitive game for the Reds?

ANSWERS ON PAGE 150

90 RED DEVIL AUTHORS

The following are the titles of books written by former players and managers. All you have to do is match the book with the correct author.

671. *Tackle Soccer This Way*   Nobby Stiles

672. *Manchester United: My Team*   Duncan Edwards

673. *Heading For Victory*   Pat Crerand

674. *Manchester United: The Quest For Glory*   Alex Ferguson

675. *Soccer My Battlefield*   Sammy McIlroy

676. *Soccer At The Top*   Tommy Docherty

677. *Touch And Go*   Bryan Robson

678. *A Year In The Life*   Steve Bruce

679. *Glory Glory Man United*   Matt Busby

680. *On Top With United*   Steve Coppell

ANSWERS ON PAGE 151

91 COSTA DEL SPAIN

681. Name the German international who has appeared for two different Spanish sides against United at Old Trafford in the European Cup Winners' Cup.

682. Can you name United's Spanish opponents in the First Round of the 1982-3 UEFA Cup?

683. Name the Argentinian striker who played for the team mentioned in the previous question.

684. Who were the Reds' first-ever Spanish opponents in European competition, and what competition did they play in?

685. United met Real Madrid in the 1968 European Cup Semi-Final. What was the score when the two teams met at Old Trafford?

686. Name the Brazilian striker who led Barcelona's attack when United met the Spanish Champions in the 1994-5 UEFA Champions League.

687. Can you name the Spanish team which put United out of the 1991-2 European Cup Winners' Cup?

688. How many Spanish sides did the Reds meet in the 1990-1 European Cup Winners' Cup competition?

689. Who were United's Spanish opponents in the 1983-4 European Cup Winners' Cup Quarter-Final?

690. Who captained the Reds' opponents referred to in the previous question?

ANSWERS ON PAGE 151

92
PICTURE QUIZ – ROUND 23

1. Where in Northern Ireland was Norman born?

2. Did Norman play for South or West Belfast Schools?

3. What age was Norman when he became the youngest player to have played in the final stages of a World Cup Final?

4. Norman won 38 caps for his country. How many of them did he win during his time at Old Trafford?

5. Against which south coast club did Norman make his United debut?

ANSWERS ON PAGE 151

93 THE 1970s – ROUND 3

691. Who provided the opposition for Bobby Charlton's Testimonial at Old Trafford in September 1972?

692. Name the former Leeds United, Birmingham City and Stoke City player who joined the Reds in November 1976.

693. Can you name the team that Tommy Docherty was managing prior to accepting the position as manager of Manchester United?

694. Name the London club thrashed 5-1 by the Reds in the Second Round of the League Cup in the 1974-5 season.

695. Which team finished Runners-up to United in the Second Division Championship of 1974-5?

696. United reached the FA Cup Finals of 1976, 1977 and 1979. Can you name the team which put them out of the FA Cup in 1978?

697. In what season during the 1970s did Nobby Stiles play his last game for the Reds?

698. Name the full-back to whom Jimmy Nicholl lost his place in the United side during season 1981-2.

699. Can you name the United defender who joined York City after leaving Old Trafford at the end of their Second Division Championship winning season?

700. How many FA Cup Semi-Finals did the Reds reach during the 1970s?

ANSWERS ON PAGE 151

94 FA CUP FINALS

701. Name the striker who scored twice for United in their 4-2 win over Blackpool in 1948.

702. Who did United meet in the 1963 Final and what was the score of the game?

703. Can you name United's full-backs in the 1976 Final?

704. Who scored the Reds' second goal in the Silver Jubilee Final of 1977?

705. In the Final of 1979, seven of the side that played had also appeared for United in the 1977 Final. Name five of the players concerned.

706. True or False – Alex Stepney was reserve goalkeeper for the Reds in the 1979 Final?

707. Who scored for United in the drawn Final of 1983 against Brighton and Hove Albion?

708. Can you name the scorer of United's winner in the 1985 Final?

709. Apart from the goalkeeper's position and substitutions, how many other changes did Alex Ferguson make to the side which drew 3-3 with Crystal Palace for the 1990 Replay?

710. In what year did the Reds last appear in front of a 100,000 Wembley crowd for a FA Cup Final?

ANSWERS ON PAGE 151

95 THE GREEN GREEN GRASS OF HOME

711. Two United players with the same surname played for the Republic of Ireland during the 1960s. Name them.

712. How many United players were included in the Northern Ireland squad for the 1986 World Cup Finals in Mexico?

713. Before joining United, Kevin Moran was already an established player in another sport. Name the previous sport in which he excelled.

714. From which club did the Reds purchase Chris McGrath in October 1976?

715. Can you name the London club from whom United signed Noel Cantwell in November 1960?

716. Against which European team did Norman Whiteside score his first international goal for Northern Ireland?

717. Where was Paul McGrath born?

718. Sammy McIlroy made his debut for Northern Ireland against Spain on 16 February 1972. In what country was the game played?

719. A United striker won his first cap for the Republic of Ireland against Denmark during the 1968-9 season. Name him.

720. Can you name the team from Northern Ireland for which Tommy Sloan played before he was transferred to United?

ANSWERS ON PAGE 151

96 PICTURE QUIZ – ROUND 24

1. What is the full title of the trophy below?

2. In what season did this trophy replace the old Division 1 Championship?

3. Who sponsored the top division before Carling took over?

4. United did the Double in 1994 and again in 1996. In which of these two years did they acquire the most Premier League points?

5. When United first won the trophy, what team finished as Runners-up?

ANSWERS ON PAGE 152

97 ALEX FERGUSON

721. Fergie was born in a famous shipbuilding area of Glasgow. Can you name it?

722. In what year did Alex become the manager of Aberdeen?

723. How many times did Aberdeen win the Scottish Premier League whilst Alex was in charge?

724. During 1986 Fergie managed three senior football teams. Name all of them.

725. How many times, up to the end of the 1996-7 season, have United finished Runners-up in the league under Alex Ferguson's management?

726. During his playing career at Falkirk, Fergie played alongside a future Scotland manager. Name him.

727. A video tape was released in 1996 to celebrate Fergie's playing and managerial career. What is it called?

728. In the summer of what year did Alex Ferguson travel to France to persuade Eric Cantona to stay at Old Trafford?

729. Who, in 1995, said, 'Alex always had a hot temper. He'd have caused a row in an empty house'?

730. What is the title of the book, written by Alex, which was published in August 1997?

ANSWERS ON PAGE 152

731. At the 1986 World Cup Finals, how many countries were represented by Manchester United players?

732. When the Reds met Everton in the 1963 FA Charity Shield, which ground staged the game?

733. Name the team which put United out of the 1996-7 Coca-Cola Cup.

734. Can you name the Scottish Club where Gordon Strachan started his professional career?

735. In the Final of what competition did United meet Manchester City in 1986?

736. A future England captain scored a hat-trick for United's Youth Team in February 1984. Name the player concerned.

737. Who scored the only goal of the game when the Reds beat Arsenal in a Premier League fixture at Old Trafford on 16 November 1996?

738. Name the two brothers who played against one another when United met Tottenham Hotspur in November 1957.

739. Can you name the first Manchester United Youth player to graduate from the FA's School Of Excellence and play successfully in league football?

740. When the Reds played Stoke City in August 1975 the opposing captains were brothers. Name them.

ANSWERS ON PAGE 152

741. In 189 appearances for the Reds I scored 128 goals and I helped England to the 1958 World Cup Finals. I lost my life in the Munich Air Disaster.

742. I was born in Johnstone, Scotland in 1958 and during my career with The Dons I won two League Championship medals, four Scottish FA Cup Winner's medals and a European Cup Winner's Cup medal.

743. I joined United in 1973 from Shrewsbury Town. I played centre-half for United and Scotland. In December 1975 I broke my leg against Sheffield Wednesday and never played First Team football for the Reds again.

744. I signed for United in 1976 and made my league debut in 1980. I was mainly used as a utility player before slotting in to the right-back position. I won two FA Cup Winner's medals with the Reds and ten full England caps.

745. I was born on 27 May 1971 and joined United from Torquay United on 1 June 1988. I left Old Trafford during the summer of 1996.

746. I joined the Reds prior to the start of the 1991-2 season. I made my league debut for United on 17 August 1991 and am a full international for my country. During the 1995-6 season I scored once for the Reds.

747. I was a Busby Babe, signing for the Reds in September 1969. I scored on my United debut in front of 63,326 fans in a famous 3-3 draw with rivals, City. I scored in the 1979 FA Cup Final. I left Old Trafford in February 1982.

748. I was born in Salford on 16 November 1974 and signed professional for the Reds on 23 January 1993 after serving my apprenticeship. I scored twice on my full United debut in a Coca-Cola Cup fixture.

749. I was born in Dublin in 1940 and spent six years at Old Trafford. In 1963 I won an FA Cup Winner's medal. After leaving United I won many honours with my new club and played in the 1975 European Cup Final.

750. I was Scotland's Player of The Year in 1987. United paid £850,000 for me in 1987 and in my first season at Old Trafford I scored 31 goals.

ANSWERS ON PAGE 152 **105**

1. Name this United star of the 1980s.

2. From which club did Ron Atkinson purchase him?

3. When he joined the Reds he did so in a £450,000-rated exchange deal which involved a United player moving in the opposite direction. Name the United player involved in the move.

4. Can you name the team he won a League Cup Winner's medal with in 1977?

5. When he left United in October 1986, which club did he sign for?

ANSWERS ON PAGE 152

101 ALL MIXED UP

All you have to do here is match United's opponents, in various competitions, with the year the event took place.

751.	Leicester City	Charity Shield	1967
752.	Southampton	FA Cup Final	1985
753.	Liverpool	Charity Shield	1983
754.	Arsenal	FA Cup Final	1948
755.	Tottenham Hotspur	Charity Shield	1963
756.	Aston Villa	League Cup Final	1985
757.	Blackpool	FA Cup Final	1957
758.	Everton	League Cup Final	1976
759.	Everton	FA Cup Final	1994
760.	Aston Villa	FA Cup Final	1948

ANSWERS ON PAGE 152

102 DIVISION TWO CHAMPIONS 1974-5

761. United won their opening league game 2-0 at London's Brisbane Road. Who did the Reds beat?

762. During the 1974-5 league campaign the Reds played four sides who, at the start of the 1997-8 season, were Premier League sides. Name three of them.

763. United's biggest win of the season was 4-0. On how many occasions did they manage this scoreline?

764. On 16 November 1974 the Reds beat Aston Villa, one of their main challengers for the Championship, 2-1 at Old Trafford. Who scored both goals for United?

765. Name the United player who scored a hat-trick in their 4-0 win over Oxford United at Old Trafford on 2 November 1974.

766. United lost only one home game all season. Can you name the victorious visitors?

767. Name the Reds striker who scored in four consecutive league games between 28 March 1975 and 5 April 1975.

768. Excluding London, how many other cities were represented by two teams in Division Two during the 1974-5 season?

769. Were United the Division's top goalscorers or did they have the meanest defence?

770. How many league games did United lose during the season?

ANSWERS ON PAGE 152

103 RED DEVIL: BOBBY CHARLTON

771. How many times did he captain England at Full International level?

772. Bobby scored twice for England in the 1966 World Cup Semi-Final. Can you name the team on the receiving end?

773. Can you name the United great who Bobby stood in for when he made his debut for the Reds?

774. Bobby holds the record for the most league appearances for United. Did he make 604, 704 or 804 league appearances?

775. How many league goals did he score for the Reds, 179, 189 or 199?

776. True or False – Bobby played in all of United's European Cup games during the 1967-8 season?

777. How many FA Youth Cup Final Winner's medals did Bobby win?

778. In what year did Bobby make his United debut?

779. Against which club did he make his last league appearance for the Reds?

780. In which Northumberland village was Bobby born?

ANSWERS ON PAGE 152

104 PICTURE QUIZ – ROUND 26

1. From which club did United purchase Stuart?

2. In his first season at Old Trafford did he score 17, 22 or 27 goals?

3. When he left Manchester United which club did he join?

4. Stuart won a Runners-up medal in 1981. Can you name the competition concerned?

5. In what year did Stuart retire from football as a result of injury, 1981, 1982 or 1983?

ANSWERS ON PAGE 153

105 SO NEAR YET SO FAR: 1991-2

781. Who were the sponsors of the English First Division in the 1991-2 season?

782. Who scored United's opening goal of their league campaign?

783. United didn't lose in the league until 26 October 1991. Name the team from Yorkshire which beat them.

784. What was the score of the first Manchester 'Derby' of the season?

785. When the Reds travelled to Elland Road for a crucial fixture in December they came away with a share of the points. Can you name the player, not normally known for his goalscoring, who netted for United in the 1-1 draw?

786. Name the team which beat the Reds at Old Trafford on Easter Monday.

787. What was the score of United's last league game of the season and who were the opposition?

788. Who was the top goalscorer for the Reds in the league?

789. Were United the league's top goalscorers for the season or the tightest defence?

790. United finished the season as Runners-up, but can you name any two of the sides which occupied third, fourth and fifth place?

ANSWERS ON PAGE 153

791. What year saw United finish nineteenth in Division 1 and win the FA Cup?

792. In what year did Denis Law join the Reds?

793. What was the year that saw Paul McGrath depart Old Trafford and Neil Webb join United from Nottingham Forest?

794. Can you recall the year that Frank O'Farrell left Leicester City to become the manager of Manchester United?

795. In what year did the Reds play two different Cup Finals at Wembley and finish Third in the First Division?

796. Can you recall the last season when 'Stretford Enders' could stand on the famous Stretford End and watch United play at Old Trafford?

797. When Manchester United were first formed they were known as Newton Heath. Name the year of formation.

798. In what year did the Reds play a Cup Final at Wembley, go out of the FA Cup in the Third Round to Tottenham Hotspur and finish Runners-up in Division 1?

799. Name the year that saw David Beckham, Nicky Butt, Gary Neville and Paul Scholes all sign as professionals for United.

800. In what year did the Reds reach the FA Cup Final, go out of the Coca-Cola Cup to a team from a lower Division and get put out of the UEFA Cup on the away goals rule?

ANSWERS ON PAGE 153

801. True or False – Gary and Philip Neville's father is called Neville Neville?

802. Name the Wigan-born goalkeeper who made three first team appearances for United in April 1972.

803. In the 1995-6 season what was the name given to the club's official mascot?

804. Can you name the group that performed United's 1994 FA Cup Final record?

805. Name the former Old Trafford hero who owns a take-away food shop close to the stadium.

806. Between April 1966 and March 1968 the Reds enjoyed a 37-game unbeaten home record. Name the first team to end this run.

807. Before joining the Reds, Roy Keane was very much in demand from another Premiership side. Name the club he turned down despite being offered rich rewards.

808. What was the name of Frank O'Farrell's assistant at Old Trafford, Malcolm Allinson, Malcolm Musgrove or Malcolm Benton?

809. What Championship medal did Arnold Muhren win in 1988?

810. Against which club did Andy Cole score his first goal at Old Trafford?

ANSWERS ON PAGE 153

1. In what year did Duncan join United from school?

2. Duncan was a product of Matt Busby's famous youth policy. How many FA Youth Cup winner's medals did he win?

3. Against which Welsh club did he make his United debut?

4. When Duncan made his full international debut for England, he was only 18 years and 183 days. Who were England's opponents?

5. How many league appearances did he make for the Reds?

ANSWERS ON PAGE 153

811. Name the player that United sold to Crewe Alexandria in February 1985.

812. United were beaten 1-0 by Glasgow Celtic at Parkhead on 25 March 1987. Can you name the Celtic player whose Testimonial it was?

813. Name the former Manchester City player who was in the United line-up for the Manchester 'Derby' game at Maine Road during the 1986-7 season.

814. Can you name the player who made his senior debut, as a substitute, for the Reds against Spartak Varna at Old Trafford on 2 November 1983?

815. A United player was playing against his former team mates in the 1985 FA Cup Final at Wembley. Name him.

816. Who were the sponsors of the English First Division during the 1985-6 season?

817. Name the player who made his league debut for the Reds against Southampton at The Dell on 3 January 1987.

818. How many crowds in excess of 50,000 watched the Reds at Old Trafford during the 1984-5 season?

819. Name either of the two players who played in 40 league games for United during the 1985-6 season.

820. The Reds suffered a shock exit in the Third Round of the 1983-4 FA Cup. Who beat them?

ANSWERS ON PAGE 153

110 IMPORTANT DATES

The following dates are all significant in the history of Manchester United. All you have to do is say what happened on the given dates from the clues beside them.

821. 27 November 1992   Inspirational signing

822. 6 November 1986   A new Dynasty begins at Old Trafford

823. 14 September 1963   Manchester witnesses a genius at work

824. 6 February 1958   The football world is in mourning

825. 24 April 1909   The first of many

826. 11 May 1996   History is made

827. 12 September 1956   United defy the football authorities

828. 26 May 1909   The birth of a legend

829. 29 May 1968   A night to remember

830. 5 April 1975   Back where we belong

ANSWERS ON PAGE 153

111 RED DEVIL: BRYAN ROBSON

831. What was the first professional club that Bryan Robson played for?

832. In how many FA Cup Finals has Bryan Robson skippered Manchester United?

833. Against which team and in what competition did he make his debut for the Reds?

834. True or False, Bryan did not play in the 1994 FA Cup Final because of an injury to his shoulder?

835. Bryan scored the Reds' only goal of their 1982-3 UEFA Cup campaign. Who were United's opponents?

836. Against which Lancashire club did Bryan make his league debut for United?

837. Can you recall the injury he sustained during the 1986 World Cup Finals in Mexico and thus forced him out of the tournament?

838. When Manchester United commenced printing the players' names on the backs of their shirts in 1994, what was Robbo's squad number?

839. Can you name the award that Manchester University gave him in 1992?

840. In 1982 Bryan scored a goal after only 27 seconds. Can you name the opposition?

ANSWERS ON PAGE 154

1. Name the London club where Alex started his professional career.

2. Can you name the team Alex left to move to Old Trafford?

3. He made his United debut on 17 September 1966 against one of the Reds' Lancashire opponents. Name the opposition.

4. Alex will always be remembered for a save he made, with normal time running out, in the 1968 European Cup Final. Whose pile-driver of a shot did he save?

5. Alex scored two goals for the Reds during his Old Trafford career. In what competition were both goals scored?

ANSWERS ON PAGE 154

841. Name any two of the four United players who were included in the PFA Premier League Team Of The Year in 1994.

842. What was the half-time score in the 1991 European Cup Winners' Cup Final?

843. During the 1994-5 season, who was United's top goalscorer?

844. Against which team did United score twice, in the opening five minutes, during an FA Cup Fifth Round game at Old Trafford on 19 February 1995?

845. Can you name the Lancashire side United beat in the Fourth Round of the Rumbelows Cup on 4 December 1991?

846. Which player scored the last goal of the 1992-3 Championship-winning season?

847. Can you name the ground where United's Reserve Team played most of their games during the 1994-5 season?

848. Name the player who reputedly did not know if he was joining Manchester United or City when he arrived in Manchester in March 1991.

849. Which team did United play in the Premiership at Old Trafford on 22 January 1994, a few days after the death of Sir Matt Busby?

850. True or False – Roy Keane played in the 1994 FA Charity Shield?

ANSWERS ON PAGE 154

114 1997-8 PRE-SEASON

851. Name the former United star and his team that won the 1996-7 Vauxhall Conference thereby gaining promotion to the Football League.

852. Who were United's opponents when Eric Cantona made his last appearance for the club?

853. Can you name the United Youth Team player who captained the England team which participated in the FIFA Coca-Cola World Youth Championship in Mexico during the summer of 1997?

854. Name one of the two other United Youth Team players who appeared in the same squad as the above named.

855. From which club did United purchase Erik Nevland?

856. How many Manchester United players represented England at Le Tournoi in France in June 1997?

857. Name the United player who scored his first goal for England at Le Tournoi and the country he scored against.

858. The Reds played Inter Milan in a pre-season friendly at the San Siro Stadium, Milan on 27 July 1997. What was the score?

859. United drew 1-1 with Inter Milan in the follow-up game to the above at Old Trafford on 30 July 1997. Who scored for the Reds?

860. What European team did the Reds play at Old Trafford on 5 August 1997?

ANSWERS ON PAGE 154

115 GENERAL – ROUND 9

861. Can you name the Italian side that United met in a special European Challenge game in May 1988?

862. What is the name of the actor who portrayed a footballer in *Yesterday's Hero,* a film believed to be centred around George Best's career?

863. Name the Arsenal defender who scored an own-goal in the match with United at Old Trafford on 2 April 1989.

864. In the late 1980s, which famous United player's mother published her autobiography entitled *Cissie*?

865. True or False – Gary Bailey scored a penalty for the Reds in their successful run in the 1984-5 FA Cup competition?

866. Can you recall the 'flower' of United's team who scored the only goal of the game when United beat Manchester City 1-0 in the 1956 FA Charity Shield?

867. In what season did Dave Sexton lead the Reds to Runners-up position in the First Division?

868. Name the on-loan goalkeeper who replaced Gary Bailey in the build-up to the 1983 FA Cup Final?

869. Which petrol company sponsored the back page of *The United Review* during the early 1970s?

870. United's top three goalscorers in the 1979-80 season were all Scottish. Name any two of them.

ANSWERS ON PAGE 154

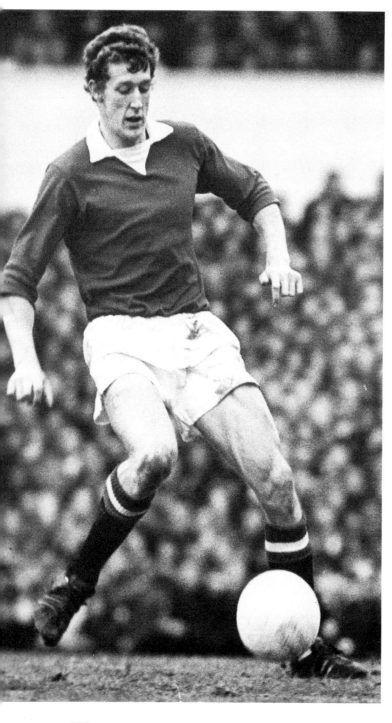

1. Name this player.

2. Before turning professional with United he obtained a degree at Manchester University. In what subject did he graduate?

3. He scored on his debut for the Reds at The Victoria Ground on 30 March 1968. Who were United's opponents?

4. For what team was he playing when he took the field in Mexico City in 1968?

5. What Yorkshire club did he join when he left Old Trafford?

ANSWERS ON PAGE 155

117 SEASON 1997-8

871. United lost their last league game of 1997. Who beat them?

872. A former United player scored in the above game. Name the player concerned.

873. Karel Poborsky left Old Trafford in December 1997. Can you name the club he signed for?

874. Name the United player who played his first Premier League game of the season on Boxing Day?

875. On 5 October 1997 United played Manchester City in a friendly for former City player Paul Lake. What was the score of the game?

876. A United Youth Team player with the surname beginning with the letter 'N' played and scored in the game. Name him.

877. At which Football League ground did United get put out of the Coca-Cola Cup?

878. During this season United announced record trading profits for the club. To the nearest £5 million, can you say how much profit the club made?

879. United played Chelsea in the Third Round of the FA Cup on 4 January 1998. What was the score of the game?

880. Who scored for the Reds in the above game?

ANSWERS ON PAGE 155

118 RED DEVIL: TEDDY SHERINGHAM

881. How much did the Reds pay Tottenham Hotspur for Teddy?

882. Name either of the two clubs that Millwall loaned him to.

883. During his career at Nottingham Forest how many goals did he score in 62 appearances, 13, 23 or 33?

884. What trophy did he win with Nottingham Forest?

885. What award did Teddy win in 1993?

886. During which season did he spearhead Tottenham's attack alongside Jurgen Klinsmann?

887. How many goals did Teddy score against the Dutch in Euro'96?

888. Can you say how many goals Teddy has scored at Old Trafford for the visiting team?

889. When he joined the Reds how many full England caps had he won, 26, 28 or 30?

890. Has he ever won a Championship medal during his professional career?

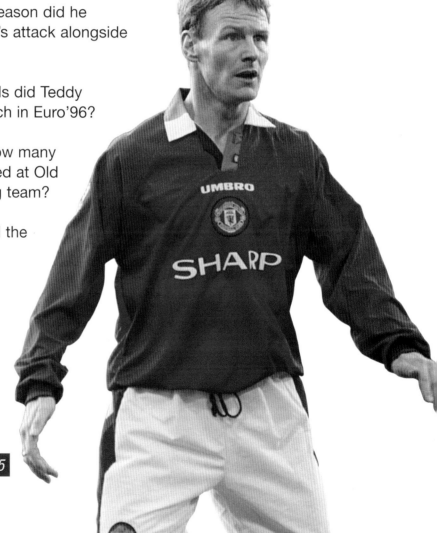

ANSWERS ON PAGE 155

119 FORMER HEROES – ROUND 3

891. True or False – Denis Law and Lou Macari were born in the same City?

892. Johnny Carey scored only one league goal during the 1952-3 season. Name the seaside club he scored against.

893. Can you name the former hero who scored a long distance free-kick against Arsenal at Old Trafford in the 1993-4 season?

894. Name the United player who became England captain in September 1982.

895. On the day of the Munich Air Disaster one of the Busby Babes sent a telegram to his landlady which read 'All flights cancelled. Flying tomorrow.' Name the Busby Babe who sent the telegram.

896. In what season did Andrei Kanchelskis make his league debut for United?

897. Name the United forward who badly damaged his knee ligaments in the 1977 FA Charity Shield.

898. Which United young player scored both United's goals in their 2-2 draw with Arsenal at Highbury on 22 March 1994?

899. Name the Northern Ireland International who scored his first goal for United in the Manchester 'Derby' game at Maine Road during the 1975-6 season.

900. Can you name the United full-back who made his league debut for the Reds against Notts County at Old Trafford on the opening day of the 1991-2 season?

ANSWERS ON PAGE 155

120 PICTURE QUIZ – ROUND 30

1. In what year did United sign Ray Wilkins?

2. True or False – Dave Sexton signed Ray for Chelsea when he was only 15 years old?

3. How much did United pay Chelsea for him, £825,000, £925,000 or £1,025,000?

4. How many FA Cup Winner's medals did he win during his Old Trafford career?

5. After leaving the Reds Ray joined AC Milan and later Glasgow Rangers. However, before moving to Scotland he played in France. Name the French club he left to move to Ibrox.

ANSWERS ON PAGE 155

MANCHESTER UNITED™

FOR THE EXPERT

121 EXPERT: LEAGUE

901. Name the player who holds the record for the longest run of consecutive league games for United.

902. Up to the end of the 1995-6 Double-winning season, no player had played for the Reds in a first team game wearing one of three numbers between 1 and 30. Can you name all three numbers?

903. Name the player who wore every outfield shirt for United, numbers 2-14, between 1984 and 1994.

904. During consecutive seasons in the 1950s, the Reds fielded the same side for the first nine league games. Which two seasons?

905. Only one United player played in all 42 league games during the fateful 1957-8 season. Name the player.

906. What is the greatest number of players used by United in a single season?

907. Two players hold the record for the most appearances for United in a single season, at 62 games. Name both of them.

908. Who is United's youngest post-war league player?

909. Who is the oldest player to have played a league game for the Reds?

910. Can you name the player who was United's captain prior to Martin Buchan taking over the armband in 1975?

ANSWERS ON PAGE 155

122 EXPERT: FA CUP

911. Up to the 1996 Final, how many FA Cup Finals have United appeared in, excluding replays?

912. Name the team which United have beaten the most often in the competition.

913. Four Reds players have each won three FA Cup Winner's medals with United. Name them.

914. United have scored four goals in the FA Cup Final on three occasions. Name the years.

915. Can you name the Irish player who appeared for United in four FA Cup Semi-Finals (1958, 1962, 1965 and 1966) but never played for the club in the Final?

916. Three United players have made their FA Cup debuts for the club in the Final. Name them.

917. Three players have scored three goals for the Reds in FA Cup Finals. Name the players.

918. Name the former United player who won a Scottish Cup Winner's medal with Glasgow Celtic in 1937, an FA Cup Winner's medal with United in1948 and an Irish Cup Winner's medal with Derry City in 1954.

919. Name the team which the Reds met in the competition in successive seasons, 1959-60, 1960-1 and 1961-2.

920. Can you name the last non-league club that United met in the competition?

ANSWERS ON PAGE 155

123 EXPERT: ERIC CANTONA

921. Against which team did Eric score twice in the game following United's exit from the European Cup in November 1993?

922. Complete the words to the following Nike billboard advertisement featuring Eric – 'We'll never forget that night at Selhurst Park. . .'

923. Eric scored the only goal of the game in Andy Cole's debut for the club. Who were the Reds' opponents?

924. When Eric returned to Selhurst Park in February 1996, for the first time since his sending off there over a year earlier, who were the opposition, what was the score of the game and how many goals, if any, did Eric score?

925. Eric scored the only goal of the game when United beat Newcastle United at St James' Park in their 1995-6 Premier League encounter. Can you remember who crossed the ball for Eric to volley home?

926. In March 1996 Eric scored in four consecutive league games. Who were United's opponents?

927. When the Reds beat Bolton Wanderers 6-0 in the Premier League on 25 February 1996, how many goals did Eric score?

928. Name the former team mate of Eric's whom he chipped a wonderful goal against in a Premier League fixture during December 1996.

929. How many trophies did the Reds win during Eric's time at Old Trafford?

930. How many goals did Eric score in 180 games for the Reds?

ANSWERS ON PAGE 156

931. United have played European matches on six English League grounds. Name them.

932. What do United's biggest wins in each of the three European competitions all have in common?

933. United have been beaten by the same side in successive European games on two occasions. Can you name the teams concerned?

934. Name the player who has played the most European games for the Reds.

935. What invitation did UEFA issue to United after the 1958 Munich Air Disaster as a measure of sympathy to those who died in the crash?

936. Name the two survivors of the Munich Air Disaster who, as a result of their injuries, never played first class football again.

937. What age was George Best when he was awarded the European Footballer Of The Year Award?

938. Who were the first club to prevent United from scoring in a European fixture at Old Trafford?

939. Who is United's all time leading goalscorer in European competition?

940. Name the club who were the first to prevent the Reds from winning a home European Cup tie.

ANSWERS ON PAGE 156

941. Name the player who scored 14 goals in seven games (includes three hat-tricks), in only 22 days at the start of the 1951-2 season.

942. Who holds the record for scoring the fastest goal for the Reds in a competitive fixture?

943. What were Newton Heath's colours (shirts and shorts) for their first two seasons in the Football League?

944. In what season have the Reds played the most competitive fixtures?

945. Who is the most expensive player to have joined United directly from local rivals Manchester City?

946. Between 1964 and 1972 United bought only three players. Name them.

947. Can you name the United player, who in the FA Cup Final of 1977, became the youngest teenager ever to have appeared in two FA Cup Finals?

948. Who was United's first £1million-plus signing?

949. Prior to Paul Ince joining Inter Milan in June 1995, who was United's record transfer sale?

950. What was significant about the £1.5 million United had to pay Nottingham Forest for Neil Webb in July 1989?

ANSWERS ON PAGE 156

951. What was significant about United's defeats in both the 1991 and 1994 League Cup Finals?

952. Name the United player who has played the most League Cup games for the Reds.

953. In the Second Round of the 1990-1 League Cup competition United played a team who were, then, bottom of the Fourth Division and who had not yet scored in the league that season. Name them.

954. When the Reds beat Arsenal 6-2 at Highbury in the Fourth Round in November 1990, Lee Sharpe scored a hat-trick. Can you name the other United scorers?

955. United's best win over two legs up to the 1996-7 competition is 7-0 (4-0 at home and 3-0 away) which came in the Second Round of the 1984-5 competition. Name the Lancashire side they defeated.

956. What is United's worst home score in the League Cup?

957. In both the 1990-1 and 1991-2 competitions United won away at the eventual English League Champions of that season. Can you name the two teams they beat?

958. In the 1970-1 competition the Reds lost to a side from the then Third Division and also lost a Wembley Final to the same side during the 1990s. Name the side concerned.

959. Can you name the United player who scored twice, in what was only his second game for the Reds, in a League Cup tie at Portsmouth in 1989?

960. Which player has scored the most goals for the Reds in the competition?

ANSWERS ON PAGE 157

127 EXPERT: TRIVIA – ROUND 2

961. Name the only United player to have scored a hat-trick for the Reds in all three major European competitions for club sides.

962. Can you name the ex-United player who scored at least one goal a season (Football League and Cup competitions) between the mid 1970s and the 1990s?

963. Apart from winning the game what else is coincidental about the last seven FA Cup Semi-Finals (up to 1996) that the Reds have played in?

964. Name the five United players who played for Scotland against England in February 1975.

965. Whilst at Old Trafford Andrei Kanchelskis won international caps for three different countries. Name the countries concerned.

966. Can you name the ex-United player who holds the record of most caps for Northern Ireland awarded to a player in an outfield position?

967. Name the two seasons that United have ended the league campaign by winning their last seven games?

968. How many times did Eric Cantona play on a losing side for the Reds in the FA Cup?

969. In the 1928-9 season United beat Newcastle United at home but lost to them away. The game ended with the same score. What was it?

970. Why did the Reds' £3.5 million purchase of Brazilian, Celio Silva, collapse in July 1997?

ANSWERS ON PAGE 157

971. Dennis Walker was the first black player to play for United but can you name the second?

972. A United hero of the 1960s married Johnny Giles' sister. Name the former hero concerned.

973. Can you name the United player who appeared as a substitute ten times during the 1974-5 season without ever making a full appearance for the first team all season?

974. Up to the end of the 1996-7 season which former United star of the 1970s holds the club record for most appearances as a substitute?

975. Name the Reds player who broke his leg making his Old Trafford debut on 2 September 1992.

976. Can you name either of the two players who at 5′ 4″ are thought to be the smallest players ever to have played for the Reds?

977. Name the player with the shortest full name to ever play for the Reds.

978. Although his playing career was effectively ended when he broke his leg in a Reserve game in December 1959, he was named as a substitute for an away game at Leicester City in 1966. Name the player concerned.

979. Can you name the player who holds the record for the most years as United captain and state the number of years he served as captain?

980. Name the player who scored four goals for the Reds, which included three penalties, in the home league game versus Aston Villa on 8 March 1950.

ANSWERS ON PAGE 157

129 EXPERT: DOUBLE WINNERS

981. How many league games did the Reds win in season 1993-4?

982. Which team did the Reds play in the FA Cup Third Round, 1993-4, and what was the score of the game?

983. On the final day of the 1995-6 season United travelled to Middlesbrough and won 3-0. Who scored for the Reds?

984. Can you name the United player who missed an open-goal in the 1995-6 FA Cup Fourth Round?

985. Who were the opposition at Old Trafford for the highest league attendance of the 1993-4 season?

986. Who did the Reds beat 2-1 at Old Trafford in the Fifth Round of the 1995-6 FA Cup on 18 February 1996?

987. During the 1995-6 season Eric Cantona was United's highest goalscorer in the league, with 14. However, two players were close behind him each scoring 11. Name them.

988. Andrei Kanchelskis scored two goals in United's 1993-4 FA Cup Sixth Round tie. Name the opposition.

989. How many teams from outside the FA Carling Premiership did the Reds meet in the 1995-6 FA Cup? Can you name them?

990. United visited Elland Road towards the end of the 1993-4 league campaign. What was the score of the game and who were the scorers?

ANSWERS ON PAGE 157

130 EXPERT: MIXED BAG

991. Three former Scottish Footballers Of The Year later signed for United. Name them.

992. At which stadium did the Reds play their last league game prior to the Munich Air Disaster on 6 February 1958?

993. Which Arab country did United visit in 1977 for the purpose of promoting British trade?

994. How many times have the Reds finished bottom of English League Division One (now known as the FA Premier League)?

995. Name the only father and son to have played for United since the Second World War.

996. What public event used to take place at Old Trafford every Sunday for a period during the 1980s?

997. Can you name the Czech Army team which the Reds played in a European Cup Winner's Cup tie during September 1983?

998. Three former United players also enjoyed two different playing spells with Manchester City. Name the players concerned.

999. Who was the first Reds player to win the Footballer Of The Year Award?

1000. Can you name the United player who scored, on his 21st birthday, against Slavia Prague on 5 August 1997?

ANSWERS ON PAGE 157

1 DOUBLE WINNERS 1993-4

1. Norwich City
2. Liverpool (30 March 1994)
3. Chelsea (1 - 0 home and away)
4. United beat Sheffield Wednesday 5 - 0
5. 2-2 (4 times: Norwich, West Ham Utd, Swindon and Arsenal
6. Charlton Athletic (Paul Parker was the player United sacrificed)
7. Oldham Athletic
8. Denis Irwin
9. Eric Cantona (18 goals)
10. Dion Dublin and Paul Ince

2 OLD TRAFFORD

11. Aston Villa beat Burnley 2-1
12. Three
13. Liverpool, 3-4
14. The FA Cup (Newcastle United v Bradford City)
15. 70,504 (27 December 1920, United lost to Aston Villa 3-1)
16. 7 January 1950 (United 4, Weymouth 0)
17. Red Star Belgrade (1-1)
18. Chelsea beat Leeds United 2-1 in a Replay after the first game at Wembley ended 2-2
19. Glasgow Celtic
20. The League Cup Finals of 1977 (second replay and 1978 (replay)

3 GENERAL – ROUND 1

21. 1,218,426
22. Nobby Stiles
23. Tim Flowers (for Blackburn Rovers at Ewood Park on 12 April 1997)
24. The first-ever game at Old Trafford under floodlights. United lost the game 0-2 to Bolton Wanderers
25. Lou Macari
26. Blackpool
27. Southampton (2-3 at Old Trafford on 8 April 1957)
28. Leeds United (1-2 on 5 December 1964)
29. West Bromwich Albion
30. Southampton (at The Dell, Lou Macari scored)

4 PICTURE QUIZ – ROUND 1

1. Choccy
2. Portsmouth
3. Aston Villa
4. Ajax Amsterdam and Nottingham Forest
5. Glasgow Celtic

5 EUROPEAN CUP WINNER'S CUP

31. 5 times (1963-4, 1977-8, 1983-4, 1990-1 and 1991-2)
32. Graeme Hogg
33. Willem II (The Netherlands, 1963-4)
34. United were not permitted to play in the 1985-6 competition as a result of the ban imposed on English clubs following the Heysel Disaster in May 1985
35. None
36. Bryan Robson
37. False, he scored in every Round except the Final
38. Pecsi Munkas (Round 1), Wrexham (Round 2)
39. Home Park, Plymouth, home of Plymouth Argyle (v St. Etienne)
40. Spurs

6 TRANSFERS – ROUND 1

41. Birmingham City
42. Torquay United
43. Ted Buckle
44. Frank O'Farrell (September 1972)
45. Shakhytor Done
46. Chicago Sting (April - August 1975)
47. Stoke City
48. Brondby
49. Portadown
50. Swindon Town as Player/Manager

7 INTERNATIONAL MIXED BAG – ROUND 1

51. Martin Buchan, Joe Jordan, Gordon McQueen and Lou Macari
52. Bobby Charlton and Denis Law
53. Johnny Carey
54. Nikola Jovanovic
55. Denis Law
56. Yugoslavia
57. Ronald Wyn Davies (1972, 1973) and Mickey Thomas (1978, 1979)
58. Jim Holton
59. Jesper Olsen, John Sivebaek and Peter Schmeichel
60. Shay Brennan, Gerry Daly, Tony Dunne, Don Givens, Ashley Grimes, Mick Martin and Paddy Roche

8 PICTURE QUIZ – ROUND 2

1. FA Cup Winner's medal 1990
2. Blackburn Rovers (in the last game of the season)
3. Darlington
4. 6′ 4″ inches
5. Southampton (at Old Trafford on 1 February 1997)

9 MATCH THE TROPHIES WITH THE YEAR THEY WERE WON

61. League Cup Winners, 1992
62. FA Cup Winners, 1909 (and 1963)
63. ECWC Winners, 1991
64. European Cup Winners, 1968
65. Division 2 Champions, 1936
66. FA Cup Winners 1963 (and 1909)
67. Division 1 Champions, 1911 (and 1952)
68. European Super Cup Winners, 1991
69. Premier League Champions, 1993
70. Division 1 Champions, 1952 (and 1911)

10 CHAMPIONS 1996-7 – ROUND 1

71. Cruyff, Johnsen, Poborsky, Solskjaer and van der Gouw
72. Phil Neville
73. 4 - 0, Cantona, Butt, Beckham and Keane
74. Nottingham Forest (4-0 on 14 September)
75. Leeds United (he put it wide of the post)
76. Aston Villa (0-0 at Villa Park, 21 September)
77. Jordi Cruyff (against West Ham United in the final game, score 2-0)
78. Leicester City (Coca-Cola Cup on 27 November 1996 and Premiership on 30 November 1996)
79. David Beckham
80. 18

11 THE 1970s – ROUND 1

81. Three (Sheff. Wed 1-0, Chelsea 3-1 and Norwich City 2-0)
82. Willie Morgan, Sammy McIlroy, Lou Macari, David McCreery, Mick Martin and Jim McCalliog
83. One (substitute appearance on 9 November 1974 away to Bristol City)
84. Wolverhampton Wanderers
85. Joe Jordan
86. Due to crowd trouble Old Trafford was closed for the opening games of the season and the Arsenal match was played at Anfield whilst the West Bromwich Albion match took place at The Victoria Ground, Stoke
87. Hillsborough
88. Martin and George Buchan
89. Bobby Charlton
90. Sheffield United

12 PICTURE QUIZ – ROUND 3

1. Billy Meredith
2. Manchester City
3. A toothpick
4. Welsh
5. Two (1908 and 1911)

13 THE LEAGUE CUP – ROUND 1

91. Andrei Kanchelskis
92. Blackpool
93. He scored United's first-ever goal in the League Cup
94. Brian Kidd
95. Stoke City (1-2 on 22 September 1993 Second Round, first leg)
96. Aston Villa (0-1 on 28 October 1992)
97. Norman Whiteside
98. Mark Hughes
99. Norwich City
100. Andrei Kanchelskis

14 LEAGUE CHAMPIONS 1992-3

101. Crystal Palace
102. Spurs (a), QPR (h), Middlesbrough (a), Liverpool (h), Blackburn (a)
103. Sheffield United (1-2 at Bramall Lane on 15 August 1992)
104. Ipswich Town (at Portman Road on 30 January 1993)
105. Peter Schmeichel, Steve Bruce and Gary Pallister
106. Sheffield Wednesday at Hillsborough
107. Coventry City
108. Hughes (15), Cantona (9), Kanchelskis (3)
109. Blackburn Rovers (last home game on 3 May 1993 when they were crowned Champions)
110. Ten (United 84 points, Aston Villa 74 points)

15 THE EUROPEAN CUP – ROUND 1

111. Real Madrid (previous European ties were played at Maine Road)
112. Gothenburg (a) and Galatasaray (h)
113. Steve Bruce
114. Shamrock Rovers (3-2 on 2 October 1957)

115. Gary Neville, Nicky Butt and David Beckham
116. Charlton and Colman
117. Graca
118. Europe, it is situated in the European part of Istanbul
119. 'Hell'
120. 6-5 (3-5 away and 3-0 home)

16 PICTURE QUIZ – ROUND 4
1. Four (1983, 1985, 1990 and 1994)
2. He scored the fastest ever goal in the final stages of the World Cup
3. Oldham Athletic (FA Cup Semi-Final Replay on 13 April 1994)
4. He became the first captain to hold aloft the FA Cup three times
5. Eggs

17 CAN YOU NAME MY PREVIOUS CLUB?
121. Mal Donaghy, Luton Town
122. Harry Gregg, Doncaster Rovers
123. Gerry Daly, Bohemians
124. Jim McCalliog, Wolves
125. David Herd, Arsenal
126. Paul McGrath, St Patrick's Athletic
127. Stuart Pearson, Hull City
128. John Gidman, Everton
129. Alex Forsyth, Partick Thistle
130. Steve Coppell, Tranmere Rovers

18 REARRANGE THE LETTERS TO FIND PAST AND PRESENT UNITED STARS
131. Bryan Robson
132. Albert Scanlon
133. Eric Cantona
134. Peter Bodak
135. Garry Birtles
136. Gary Pallister
137. Nobby Stiles
138. Paul Parker
139. Mark Hughes
140. Pat Crerand

19 MATCH THE PLAYER WITH THE CLUB UNITED BOUGHT HIM FROM
141. Terry Gibson, Coventry City
142. Noel Cantwell, West Ham United
143. Martin Buchan, Aberdeen
144. Alan Brazil, Tottenham Hotspur
145. Chris Turner, Sunderland

146. Albert Quixall, Sheffield Wednesday
147. Mike Phelan, Norwich City
148. Willie Morgan, Burnley
149. Stewart Houston, Brentford
150. Peter Barnes, Leeds United

20 PICTURE QUIZ – ROUND 5
1. Liam O'Brien
2. Ron Atkinson
3. Newcastle United
4. He was sent off in the first minute against Southampton on 3 January 1987
5. Dublin

21 UNITED IN EUROPE – ROUND 1
151. Rotterdam
152. Torpedo Moscow (4-3 on penalties)
153. Denis Law (28 goals from 33 appearances)
154. No.7 (John Aston wore No.11)
155. A crowd of 130,000 attended the game, the highest attendance ever for a United game
156. Paul Ince
157. Dundee United
158. Tottenham Hotspur (1963-4 ECWC) and Everton (1964-5 Inter-Cities Fairs Cup)
159. Paul Parker and Gary Neville
160. Bill Foulkes and Bobby Charlton

22 WHO AM I? – ROUND 1
161. Ray Wilkins
162. Norman Whiteside
163. Neil Webb
164. Lee Sharpe
165. Lou Macari
166. Paul Ince
167. Ryan Giggs
168. Dion Dublin
169. George Best
170. Denis Law

23 GENERAL – ROUND 2
171. Andy Cole
172. Bryan Robson
173. Clayton Blackmore
174. *Bubbly* by George Best
175. Denis Irwin and Anders Limpar
176. 1976-7
177. Alan and Derek Brazil
178. Leicester City on 27 October 1993
179. Brian McClair
180. Sir Matt Busby

24 PICTURE QUIZ – ROUND 6

1. Four times (1967-8, 1969-70, 1970-1 and 1971-2)
2. He threw mud at the referee
3. Hibernian
4. None
5. 1985

25 FA CUP – ROUND 1

181. Bournemouth (2-0)
182. Norman Whiteside
183. Southampton (2-2 a.e.t., Southampton won 4-2 on penalties)
184. Jack Rowley
185. Sheffield Wednesday
186. Fulham
187. Frank Stapleton
188. Liverpool
189. At the Crystal Palace (not Selhurst Park)
190. Everton

26 DOUBLE DOUBLE WINNERS – ROUND 1

191. Nottingham Forest on 28 April 1996 (last home game of the season)
192. Nicky Butt and Eric Cantona
193. Reading [a]
194. Phil (Gary came on as a substitute for David Beckham)
195. Peter Schmeichel (he played 36 of the 38 Premiership matches)
196. Villa Park, Birmingham
197. Manchester City 2, Manchester United 3
198. Reading
199. Blackburn Rovers on 28 August 1995 (at Ewood Park)
200. Ian Rush

27 RED DEVIL: ERIC CANTONA

201. Goalkeeper
202. Auxerre
203. Sheffield Wednesday
204. 'wife', 'marriage'
205. Jim Leighton (playing for Scotland)
206. Rimbaud
207. Nike
208. Swindon Town and Arsenal
209. £1.2 million
210. Ryan Giggs

28 PICTURE QUIZ – ROUND 7

1. Colin Gibson
2. Aston Villa
3. West Bromwich Albion
4. £275,000
5. Two (West Ham Utd [a] and Derby County [h])

29 DOUBLE WINNERS 1993-4 – ROUND 2

211. Norwich City (2-0 at Carrow Road)
212. Two (versus Wimbledon and Oldham Athletic)
213. Oldham Athletic (he came on for Paul Parker in the first Semi-Final)
214. Norwich City on the opening day of the season
215. Newcastle United
216. 92
217. Blackburn Rovers (0-2 away)
218. Nine (Sheffield United, Aston Villa, Southampton, Sheffield Wednesday, Spurs, Everton, QPR, Man. City and Oldham)
219. Brian McClair
220. Seven (Sheff. Utd.,Norwich, Wimbledon, Charlton Athletic, Oldham, [twice], and Chelsea)

30 THE 1990s IN THE LEAGUE

221. Chelsea
222. Alan Wilkie
223. Queens Park Rangers
224. Andrei Kanchelskis, Eric Cantona and Andy Cole
225. Eric Cantona (for Leeds against Spurs)
226. 2-2
227. Four
228. Viral Meningitis
229. Queens Park Rangers
230. All 21

31 IN THE HOT SEAT – UNITED MANAGERS

231. Norwich City
232. Frank O'Farrell
233. Jimmy Murphy
234. Derby County
235. Archie Knox;
236. Ernest Mangnall
237. Eight-Matt Busby (1945-69), Jimmy Murphy (Feb. 1958-Aug. 1958), Wilf McGuinness (1969-70), Frank O'Farrell (1971-2), Tommy Docherty (1972-7), Dave

Sexton (1977-81), Ron Atkinson (1981-6), Alex Ferguson (1986-present)
238. Alex Ferguson
239. Clarence Hilditch (October 1926-April 1927)
240. Jimmy Hill

32 PICTURE QUIZ – ROUND 8
1.   Ron Atkinson and Alex Ferguson
2.   1985 FA Cup Winner's medal
3.   He worked in a bank
4.   Bordeaux
5.   Stoke City

33 1994-5 LEAGUE GAMES
241. Mark Hughes in the first game of the season versus QPR at Old Trafford on 20 August 1994
242. Steve Bruce
243. Brian McClair
244. Leeds United (1-2 at Elland Road on 11 September 1994)
245. Nottingham Forest (United lost 1-2)
246. Newcastle United
247. Eric Cantona and Mark Hughes
248. Eric Cantona-4, Denis Irwin-1 (Cantona was serving his ban)
249. Cole-5, Hughes-2, Keane-1 and Ince-1
250. Brian McClair against West Ham United at Upton Park on 14 May 1995

34 RED DEVIL: GEORGE BEST
251. 1963
252. Footballer of the Year and European Footballer of the Year
253. Five (1968-72 inclusive)
254. 2
255. 2
256. 6
257. 6
258. 'El Beatle'
259. 1974 (New Year's Day)
260. L A Aztecs

35 GENERAL – ROUND 3
261. They have all played for Manchester City
262. 3-1 to Celtic
263. 31
264. M. E.
265. He designed Old Trafford (opened 1910)
266. 54,750
267. Les Sealey

268. 1960 (at Bolton Wanderers on 1 October)
269. Hi-Tec
270. Nineteenth

36 PICTURE QUIZ – ROUND 9
1.   He played a round of golf
2.   Waterford
3.   FIFA XI
4.   1964
5.   He was in hospital recovering from a leg injury

37 LEAGUE POSITIONS
271. 1970-1, 8th
272. 1972-3, 18th
273. 1973-4, 21st
274. 1975-6, 3rd
275. 1976-7, 6th
276. 1977-8, 10th
277. 1978-9, 9th
278. 1979-80, 2nd
279. 1983-4, 4th
280. 1986-7, 11th

38   1980s – ROUND 1
281. They drew most of their games (18 in total)
282. John Gidman and Frank Stapleton
283. Laurie Cunningham
284. Luton Town
285. Norman Whiteside
286. Watford
287. Notts County (a)
288. Garry Birtles (Nottingham Forest)
289. Joe Jordan with 15 goals
290. Billy Garton, Paul McGrath, Gordon McQueen and Kevin Moran

39 SENDINGS OFF
291. None
292. George Best (United beat Chelsea 3-2)
293. He handled the ball on the goal-line
294. Paul Parker
295. Arsenal
296. Nobby Stiles
297. George Best
298. Peter Willis
299. 2
300. Mark Hughes

40 PICTURE QUIZ – ROUND 10
1. Auxerre, Martigues, Olympique Marseilles, Bordeaux, Montpellier and Nimes
2. Blackburn Rovers (FA Premier League, 22 January 1995)
3. Lee Sharpe
4. 43
5. 30 (Born 24 May 1966, Retired 18 May 1997)

41 GENERAL – ROUND 4
301. Panini
302. Stoke City
303. Red Star Belgrade
304. No.2
305. Brian Greenhoff
306. Ian Greaves
307. Stewart Houston
308. 2
309. Ipswich Town
310. Joe Jordan (manager of Bristol City)

42 TELEVISION STARS
311. Ray Wilkins
312. Tottenham Hotspur (United won 4-2)
313. 1986
314. Luton Town
315. Mark Bosnich
316. Nobby Stiles
317. Newcastle United (at St James' Park)
318. 1969
319. TV AM
320. Southampton away. United won 1-0

43 FORMER HEROES – ROUND 1
321. Bill Foulkes
322. Stuart Pearson
323. Aston Villa at Villa Park on 13 December 1989
324. Fulham
325. Les Sealey
326. Bobby Charlton
327. Harry Gregg and Bill Foulkes
328. Joe Jordan
329. Norwich City (he left Norwich to join Cambridge United)
330. Dennis Walker (debut: 20 May 1963)

44 PICTURE QUIZ – ROUND 11
1. Gillingham
2. 13
3. Dave Watson
4. He conceded a penalty and broke his nose
5. League Cup Winner's medal (with Norwich City)

45 THE 1970s – ROUND 2
331. Jock Stein
332. Stoke City (0-1)
333. Stuart Pearson
334. Sheffield Wednesday (away)
335. Frank O'Farrell
336. Hull City
337. Two (Liverpool and Leicester City)
338. Three
339. 1977-8
340. 32

46 LEAGUE CUP – ROUND 2
341. Newcastle United
342. Arsenal Stadium, Highbury
343. Ronnie Whelan
344. Middlesbrough
345. Ryan Giggs
346. Steve Pears
347. Four – Liverpool, Arsenal, Southampton and Leeds United
348. 1960-1
349. Oxford United
350. All Blue

47 THE GREY KIT 1995-6
351. The black kit
352. Aston Villa (at Villa Park)
353. Aston Villa won 3-1
354. Five (away to Aston Villa, Arsenal, Nottingham Forest, Liverpool and Southampton)
355. One
356. Away to Nottingham Forest
357. David Beckham, Eric Cantona and Ryan Giggs
358. Sharp Viewcam
359. White
360. It was claimed that the players couldn't pick each other out against the background of the crowd!

48 PICTURE QUIZ – ROUND 12
1. Gerry Daly
2. Arsenal (at Highbury on 25 August 1973)
3. Tommy Docherty and Derby County
4. 46
5. Bohemians (of Dublin)

49 MANCHESTER 'DERBY' GAMES

361. Gordon Hill
362. Mickey Thomas
363. Eric Cantona
364. Paul Bielby
365. It was the first Manchester 'Derby' game played after the Seccond World War
366. 1960 (31 December at Old Trafford, United 5, City 1)
367. 2-1 to United
368. Ron Atkinson
369. 2-0 (Robson and Reid o.g.)
370. Tommy and Michael Docherty

50 ERIC THE KING

371. 9
372. 1994
373. An Indian brave
374. 180
375. Four (three with United, 1993, 1994 and 1996 and one with Leeds in 1992)
376. 1993-4 with 25 goals
377. The Football Writers' Association Player of The Year
378. 80
379. 1 (on his United debut at Old Trafford against Man City on 6 December 1992)
380. 11% (or approximately 1 in every 10 games)

51 RED DEVIL: PETER SCHMEICHEL

381. False, he was suspended. Les Sealey was in goal
382. Rotor Volgograd
383. Galatasaray
384. One
385. Notts County (at Old Trafford on 17 August 1991)
386. 1992-3
387. Gladsaxe (on 18 November 1963. He was signed from Brondby)
388. One (versus York City [a])
389. Kevin Pilkington
390. The goalposts. It's part of his pre-match superstition.

52 PICTURE QUIZ – ROUND 13

1. Everton (at Old Trafford on 2 March 1991)
2. A League Cup Winner's medal on 12 April 1992 (He won a FA Youth Cup Winner's medal the following month)
3. He became the first player to win two successive PFA Young Player of the Year Awards
4. AC Milan
5. Joseph

53 SIR MATT BUSBY

391. FA Cup
392. Manchester City
393. Jimmy Delaney
394. The 1948 FA Cup
395. 5 (1952, 1956, 1957, 1965 and 1967)
396. Four times (1948, 1957, 1958 and 1963). Winners in 1948 and 1963
397. False. United finished Runners-up seven times (1947, 1948, 1949, 1951, 1959, 1964 and 1968)
398. 1945
399. None. They were winners in 1952, 1956 and 1957 and Joint-Holders in 1965 and 1967;
400. He received a Knighthood from the Queen

54 WHAT WAS THE YEAR? – ROUND 1

401. 1977
402. 1982
403. 1988
404. 1982 (August)
405. 1989 and 1991
406. 1987
407. 1972
408. 1966
409. 1930s
410. 1992

55 GENERAL – ROUND 5

411. No.4
412. Leeds United (60,025 on 9 February 1974, Leeds won 2-0)
413. Tommy Taylor
414. Manchester United 4, Nottingham Forest 0
415. Wimbledon (at Selhurst Park on 9 May 1993)
416. Brighton and Hove Albion. They arrived by helicopter
417. Jim Holton and Lou Macari (Macari scored)
418. Charlie Nicholas (he joined Arsenal)
419. Andrei Kanchelskis (Robson didn't play)
420. Bill Foulkes

56 PICTURE QUIZ – ROUND 14

1. Remi Moses
2. None
3. West Bromwich Albion
4. £600,000 (some records will show £650,000)
5. Swansea City (at Old Trafford on 19 September 1981)

57 INTERNATIONAL MIXED BAG – ROUND 2

421. Cardiff
422. The Great Britain Olympic Team
423. One
424. Roy Keane and Denis Irwin
425. Norman Whiteside
426. False, he won it whilst at Glasgow Celtic
427. None
428. The Republic of Ireland
429. Ray Wilkins
430. 1983

58 EUROPEAN CUP – ROUND 2

431. Waterford
432. Brussels, Belgium
433. 3-2 (United won 3-2 at home and drew 0-0 away)
434. Alex Stepney
435. ASK Vorwarts (they met HJK Helsinki in the Preliminary Round)
436. 3-3
437. Charlton and Coluna
438. Partizan Belgrade (United lost 0-2 away and won the home leg 1-0)
439. Malta
440. Dennis Viollet

59 FA CUP – ROUND 2

441. Maine Road
442. Manchester City
443. George Best with 21 goals (Charlton scored 19)
444. Jackie Blanchflower
445. Martin Buchan (Winner with Aberdeen in 1970 and with United in 1977)
446. 1977, 1983 and 1985
447. David Gaskell
448. One (in 1985)
449. West Bromwich Albion
450. Wrexham

60 PICTURE QUIZ – ROUND 15

1. The No.11 shirt
2. 106
3. Preston North End
4. 1966
5. 1958

61 UNITED IN EUROPE – ROUND 2

451. 1-1
452. Raba Vasas Eto Gyor
453. Sweden
454. Five-Juventus (h & a), Fenerbahce (h), Borussia Dortmund (h & a)
455. Mark Hughes, Arnold Muhren and McGinnis (o.g.)
456. FC Porto (lost 0-4 away and won 5-2 at home)
457. Athletic Bilbao
458. Rapid Vienna
459. 1-1 (United lost on the away goals rule)
460. Juventus, Rapid Vienna and Fenerbahce

62 FORMER HEROES – ROUND 2

461. Sammy McIlroy
462. Denis Law (£115,000 from Torino on 12 July 1962)
463. Mark Hughes
464. Gordon McQueen
465. Pat Dunne
466. Mike Duxbury
467. Martin Buchan
468. Nobby Lawton
469. Harry Gregg
470. Hogg, Hughes, Olsen, McGrath and Strachan

63 FRIENDLIES AND TESTIMONIALS

471. David Sadler
472. Everton (at Old Trafford)
473. Toronto (the Toronto Cup)
474. Glasgow Celtic (1-1 draw at Parkhead)
475. Eusebio
476. David O'Leary
477. Norway and Sweden
478. The Scottish FA refused Celtic permission to participate in the game
479. Aberdeen
480. Real Madrid

64 PICTURE QUIZ – ROUND 16
1. Bayern Munich
2. The League Cup (substitute for Whiteside against Port Vale on 26 October 1983)
3. England
4. 1984-5 (he scored 16 goals)
5. Spain

65 CHAMPIONS 1996-7 – ROUND 2
481. Aston Villa
482. Two (Leicester City away 2-2 and Middlesbrough at home 3-3)
483. Gary Kelly (for bringing Giggs down in the area)
484. Peter Reid (Sunderland were relegated on the final day of the season)
485. Wimbledon (2-1)
486. Newcastle United (0-5 at St James'Park on 20 October)
487. Keane, Neville (Gary) and Solskjaer
488. Aston Villa
489. Nottingham Forest, eight goals (4 -1 at home and 4-0 away)
490. 75

66 IRISH CONNECTION
491. Kispest Honved
492. Four-Jimmy Nicholl, Sammy McIlroy, David McCreery and Tommy Jackson
493. Mick Martin
494. Six
495. Noel Cantwell
496. Norman Whiteside
497. Sammy McIlroy
498. Tulsa Roughnecks
499. Sammy McIlroy
500. Johnny Giles (one with United, four with Leeds United)

67 DOUBLE DOUBLE WINNERS – ROUND 2
501. Six
502. Andy Cole
503. Manchester United 2, Newcastle United 0. Scorers: Cole and Keane
504. Seven
505. Middlesbrough (he punched Fjortoft)
506. Manchester City
507. Liverpool (the game ended 2-2)
508. Southampton
509. Liverpool (0-2 on 17 December 1996) and Leeds (1-3 on 24 December 1996)

510. Three (Sunderland [a], Reading [a] and Southampton [h])

68 PICTURE QUIZ – ROUND 17
1. Leeds United (at Old Trafford)
2. 55 yards
3. Tottenham Hotspur (FA Cup and FA Carling Premiership)
4. Moldova (a)
5. Rapid Vienna (h) and Fenerbahce (a)

69 RED DEVIL: GARY PALLISTER
511. True
512. The PFA Player of the Year Award
513. Ramsgate, Kent
514. Wrexham (1990-1 ECWC)
515. 1988 (30 August)
516. Newcastle United (away on 29 October 1994) and Southampton (away on 31 December 1994)
517. None
518. £2.3 million
519. Two (both headers)
520. True (Pallister 36, Johnsen 37 and May 38)

70 UP FRONT
521. Cambridge United
522. Joe Jordan (for Scotland)
523. 'Pancho'
524. Port Vale (at Vale Park)
525. Garth Crooks
526. Craig Forrest
527. No.10
528. None
529. Cyprus
530. Peter Davenport

71 FLOWERS OF SCOTLAND
531. Gordon Strachan
532. Portsmouth
533. Gordon Banks
534. Alex Dawson
535. Paddy Crerand
536. He was a miner
537. Bellshill
538. Jim Leighton
539. Scott Duncan
540. Willie Morgan

72 PICTURE QUIZ – ROUND 18

1. St Patrick's Athletic
2. One (1985)
3. Coca-Cola Cup Final (with Aston Villa)
4. 1989
5. 1985

73 INTERNATIONAL DEBUTS

541. Nicky Butt, Mexico
542. Eric Cantona, West Germany
543. Andy Cole, Uruguay
544. Ryan Giggs, Belgium
545. Denis Irwin, Morocco
546. Roy Keane, Chile
547. Gary Neville, Japan
548. Ole Gunnar Solskjaer, Jamaica
549. Brian McClair, Luxembourg
550. Phil Neville, China

74 FOREIGN AFFAIRS

551. Jordi Cruyff
552. Peter Schmeichel
553. Arnold Muhren
554. Ole Gunnar Solskjaer
555. Eric Cantona
556. Jesper Olsen
557. Andrei Kanchelskis
558. Ronny Johnsen
559. Nikola Jovanovic
560. Karel Poborsky

75 THE 1980s – ROUND 2

561. Paul McGrath
562. Bryan Robson and Mark Hughes
563. Ron Atkinson
564. Mark Higgins
565. John Sivebaek
566. Three
567. Alex Ferguson after the sacking of Ron Atkinson
568. Remi Moses (after a training ground bust-up)
569. West Bromwich Albion
570. Tommy Cavanagh

76 PICTURE QUIZ – ROUND 19

1. Blackpool (at Old Trafford)
2. £56,000
3. Glasgow (The Gorbals)
4. Northampton Town
5. Two (1964-5 and 1966-7)

77 YOUNG GUNS

571. Chris Casper, Michael Clegg, Andy Cole and Jordi Cruyff
572. Bolton Wanderers (at Old Trafford)
573. Bradford City
574. Nicky Butt conceded and Alessandro Del Piero scored
575. Ole Gunnar Solskjaer (versus Blackburn Rovers at Old Trafford)
576. David Beckham
577. West Ham United (away)
578. Nicky Butt
579. Pat McGibbon
580. Michael Appleton

78 UNITED v LIVERPOOL

581. 3-3
582. Colin Gibson
583. Rumbelows Cup (League Cup)
584. Bruce, Hughes and Sharpe
585. John Barnes
586. Bruce, Giggs and Irwin
587. Once (1984-5 Semi-Final)
588. Willie Morgan, Ian Ure and Ron Yeats (o.g.)
589. Ronnie Whelan
590. Jimmy Greenhoff

79 NICKNAMES

591. Nobby Stiles, 'Happy'
592. Arthur Albiston, 'Chips'
593. Mark Hughes, 'Sparky'
594. Jack Rowley, 'Gunner'
595. Lou Macari, 'The Judge'
596. Denis Law, 'The King'
597. Gordon Hill, 'Merlin'
598. Paul McGrath, 'The Black Pearl Of Inchicore'
599. Alex Dawson, 'The Black Prince'
600. George Best, 'El Beatle'

80 PICTURE QUIZ – ROUND 20

1. Fort Lauderdale, Atlanta Chiefs and Minnesota Strikers
2. Archie Knox
3. Preston North End
4. Arsenal
5. 19

81 RED DEVIL: BRIAN McCLAIR

601. 1987
602. All 42
603. The Coca-Cola Cup
604. 1986, Andy Roxborough
605. Derby County
606. False, he scored United's fourth goal
607. 3
608. Motherwell
609. 1992
610. George Best (28 goals during season 1967-8)

82 TRANSFERS – ROUND 2

611. AC Milan
612. Ajax Amsterdam
613. Ted MacDougall
614. Bologna
615. Brentford
616. Arthur Graham
617. Billy Bremner
618. Manchester City
619. Birmingham City
620. Coventry City

83 WELSH DRAGONS

621. Wyn Davies
622. Uruguay
623. Jimmy Murphy
624. None (Wales didn't qualify for the Finals)
625. Mickey Thomas
626. Neath (23 September 1964)
627. Alan Davies
628. Tottenham Hotspur (at White Hart Lane on 19 September 1992)
629. Colin Webster (v Czechoslovakia in 1957)
630. Mickey Thomas

84 PICTURE QUIZ – ROUND 21

1. Cork (31 October 1965)
2. 1990 (signed professional on 8 June 1990)
3. One (on the opening day of the season at Wimbledon)
4. Alex Ferguson
5. Joe Royle (manager of Oldham Athletic)

85 SILVERWARE

631. 1953-7 inclusive
632. The Anglo-Italian Cup
633. The Watney Cup
634. Everton (2-0)
635. Argentina
636. Screen Sports Super Cup

637. Once only (in 1968 when they were the European Cup Winners
638. Jim McCalliog
639. Tottenham Hotspur (Aggregate score 2-2. United won 4-3 on penalties)
640. Ray Wilkins

86 GENERAL – ROUND 6

641. Manchester City
642. Gary Bailey
643. False (he didn't play)
644. George Best
645. 1991
646. Black (with a Red and White stripe)
647. Glasgow Rangers
648. Leeds United (0-1 at Burnden Park, Bolton on 26 March 1970)
649. 'Supersub'
650. Jesper Olsen (he used to play for PSV's rivals, Ajax Amsterdam)

87 INTERNATIONAL MIXED BAG – ROUND 3

651. Arnold Muhren
652. Ukraine (formerly part of the USSR)
653. Glenn Hysen (he joined Liverpool)
654. Niall Quinn of the Republic of Ireland
655. Bobby Charlton, Nobby Stiles and John Connelly
656. AC Milan and Brazil
657. None (he won them whilst at Arsenal);
658. Raimond van der Gouw
659. Ole Gunnar Solskjaer and Ronny Johnsen
660. Bryan Robson

88 PICTURE QUIZ – ROUND 22

1. Blackburn Rovers (on 1 July 1994)
2. Queens Park Rangers
3. Oldham (24 June 1970). David supported Manchester City.
4. FC Porto (at Old Trafford on 5 March 1997), United won 4-1
5. Mexico

89 RED DEVIL: MARK HUGHES

661. 1.8 million
662. Wrexham (on 1 November 1963)
663. Arsenal (at Old Trafford on 22 March 1995, FA Carling Premiership)
664. His equaliser in the 1994 FA Cup Semi-Final against Oldham Athletic (painting by Pascal Farrell)
665. False (he scored United's third goal,

McClair got the fourth)
666. Newcastle United (at St James' Park, he got hurt in a collision with Pavel Srnicek and was stretchered off)
667. Midfield
668. Three (two in the 1990 Final and one in the 1994 Final)
669. Gary Lineker
670. Everton (in the 1995 FA Cup Final at Wembley on 20 May 1995)

90 RED DEVIL AUTHORS
671. *Tackle Soccer This Way*, Duncan Edwards
672. *Manchester United: My Team*, Sammy McIlroy
673. *Heading For Victory*, Steve Bruce
674. *Manchester United: The Quest For Glory*, Tommy Docherty
675. *Soccer My Battlefield*, Nobby Stiles
676. *Soccer At The Top*, Matt Busby
677. *Touch And Go*, Steve Coppell
678. *A Year In The Life*, Alex Ferguson
679. *Glory Glory Man United*, Bryan Robson
680. *On Top With United*, Pat Crerand

91 COSTA DEL SPAIN
681. Bernd Schuster (Barcelona and Atletico Madrid)
682. Valencia CF (United drew the home leg 0-0 and lost 1-2 away)
683. Mario Kempes (World Cup Winner in 1978)
684. Athletic Bilbao (United beat the Spaniards 6-5 on aggregate in the 1956-7 European Cup Quarter-Final and lost to Real Madrid in the Semi-Final, 3-5 on aggregate)
685. Manchester United 1, Real Madrid 0
686. Romario
687. Atletico Madrid (United were the holders but lost 0-3 away and could only draw 1-1 in the home leg of the Second Round)
688. One (they beat Barcelona 2-1 in the Final in Rotterdam)
689. Barcelona (United lost the first leg 0-2 in Spain and won the home leg 3-0)
690. Diego Maradona

92 PICTURE QUIZ – ROUND 23
1. Belfast
2. West Belfast Schools
3. 17
4. 36
5. Brighton and Hove Albion (at the Goldstone Ground on 24 April 1982)

93 THE 1970s – ROUND 3
691. Glasgow Celtic
692. Jimmy Greenhoff
693. Scotland
694. Charlton Athletic (at Old Trafford on 11 September 1974)
695. Aston Villa
696. West Bromwich Albion (Fourth Round Replay, 1-1 (h) and 2-3 (a) a.e.t.)
697. 1970-1
698. John Gidman
699. Steve James
700. Four (1970, 1976, 1977 and 1979)

94 FA CUP FINALS
701. Jack 'Gunner' Rowley
702. Leicester City. United were the underdogs but won 3-1
703. Alex Forsyth and Stewart Houston
704. Jimmy Greenhoff (Lou Macari's shot struck Greenhoff on the chest on the way to the net and he was credited with the winning goal)
705. Nicholl, Albiston, McIlroy, Buchan, Coppell, Greenhoff (J) and Macari
706. False (he left United in February 1979 and joined Dallas Tornado in the NASL)
707. Stapleton and Wilkins
708. Norman Whiteside
709. None (in the first game Blackmore came on as a sub for Martin and Robins came on for Pallister)
710. The Final of 1985 versus Everton

95 THE GREEN GREEN GRASS OF HOME
711. Pat Dunne (Goalkeeper) and Tony Dunne (Full-back)
712. One (Norman Whiteside)
713. Gaelic Football
714. Tottenham Hotspur
715. West Ham United
716. Austria (on 21 September 1983)
717. London (Ealing)
718. England (Boothferry Park, Hull, because of the unrest in Northern Ireland)
719. Don Givens
720. Ballymena United

96 PICTURE QUIZ – ROUND 24
1. The FA Carling Premiership or The FA Carling Premiership Trophy
2. The 1992-3 season
3. Barclays
4. 1994 – 92 points (82 points in 1996)
5. Aston Villa

97 ALEX FERGUSON
721. Govan
722. 1978
723. Three
724. Aberdeen, Scotland (1986 World Cup) and Manchester United
725. Three (1988, 1992 and 1995)
726. Andy Roxborough
727. *Alex Ferguson CBE, The Official Story*
728. 1995
729. Martin Ferguson (Alex's younger brother)
730. *A Will To Win: The Manager's Diary*

98 GENERAL – ROUND 7
731. 4 (Denmark, England, Northern Ireland & Scotland)
732. Goodison Park (home of Everton, the 1962-3 League Champions)
733. Leicester City (0-2 at Filbert Street on 27 November 1996)
734. Dundee
735. The FA Youth Cup Final (United lost 1-3 on aggregate)
736. David Platt (United allowed him to leave Old Trafford without signing him)
737. Nigel Winterburn (it was an own-goal)
738. Jackie Blanchflower (United) and Danny Blanchflower (Spurs)
739. Mark Robins
740. Brian Greenhoff (of United) and Jimmy Greenhoff (of Stoke City)

99 WHO AM I? – ROUND 2
741. Tommy Taylor
742. Jim Leighton
743. Jim Holton
744. Mike Duxbury
745. Lee Sharpe
746. Peter Schmeichel
747. Sammy McIlroy
748. Paul Scholes
749. Johnny Giles
750. Brian McClair

100 PICTURE QUIZ – ROUND 25
1. John Gidman
2. Everton (August 1981)
3. Mickey Thomas
4. Aston Villa (they beat Everton, at the third attempt, 3-2 at Old Trafford)
5. Manchester City

101 ALL MIXED UP
751. Leicester City, FA Cup Final, 1963
752. Southampton, FA Cup Final, 1976
753. Liverpool, League Cup Final, 1983
754. Arsenal, Charity Shield, 1948
755. Tottenham Hotspur, Charity Shield, 1967
756. Aston Villa, FA Cup Final, 1957
757. Blackpool, FA Cup Final, 1948
758. Everton, Charity Shield, 1985
759. Everton, FA Cup Final, 1985
760. Aston Villa, League Cup Final, 1994

102 DIVISION TWO CHAMPIONS 1974-5
761. Orient
762. Aston Villa, Bolton Wanderers, Sheffield Wednesday and Southampton
763. Four times (Millwall, Oxford United, Cardiff City and Blackpool-all at Old Trafford)
764. Gerry Daly
765. Stuart Pearson
766. Bristol City (0-1 on 1 February 1975)
767. Lou Macari (Bristol Rovers [a] 28 March 1975, York City [h] 29 March 1975, Oldham Athletic [h] 31 March 1975 and Southampton [h] 5 April 1975)
768. Three-Birmingham (Aston Villa and West Bromwich Albion), Bristol (City and Rovers) and Nottingham (County and Forest)
769. They had the meanest defence conceding 30 (Aston Villa were the top scorers with 69, United were close behind on 66)
770. Seven (Norwich City, Bristol City [h] and [a], Hull City, Oldham Athletic, Oxford United and Aston Villa)

103 RED DEVIL: BOBBY CHARLTON
771. Three
772. Portugal
773. Tommy Taylor
774. 604 (includes 2 substitute appearances)
775. 199
776. True
777. Two (1954-5 and 1955-6)

778. 1956 (6 October versus Charlton Athletic)
779. Chelsea (at Stamford Bridge on 28 April 1973)
780. Ashington

104 PICTURE QUIZ – ROUND 26
1. Hull City
2. 17
3. West Ham United (for £220,000 in August 1979)
4. League Cup (Liverpool beat West Ham Utd 2-1 after a replay)
5. 1982 (he made a comeback in 1985)

105 SO NEAR YET SO FAR: 1991-2
781. Barclays Bank
782. Mark Hughes (versus Notts County on opening day)
783. Sheffield Wednesday (2-3 at Hillsborough)
784. 0-0 (at Maine Road on 16 November 1991)
785. Neil Webb
786. Nottingham Forest (1-2 on 20 April 1992)
787. Manchester United 3, Tottenham Hotspur 1 (at Old Trafford on 2 May 1992)
788. Brian McClair with 18 goals (Mark Hughes scored 11)
789. They had the tightest defence conceding only 33 goals (Arsenal were the league's top scorers with 81, United hit 63)
790. Third: Sheffield Wednesday, Fourth: Arsenal, Fifth: Manchester City

106 WHAT WAS THE YEAR? – ROUND 2
791. 1963 (United beat Leicester City 3-1 in the FA Cup Final)
792. 1962 (12 July 1962)
793. 1989
794. 1971 (June)
795. 1983 (Milk Cup and FA Cup Finals)
796. 1991-2
797. 1878 (they became Manchester United in 1902 following the club's bankruptcy)
798. 1968 (United beat Benfica in the 1968 European Cup Final at Wembley and Manchester City won the League)
799. 1993 (all four of them signed professional on 23 January 1993)
800. 1995 (United lost the 1995 FA Cup Final 0-1 to Everton, Rotor Volgograd drew 2-2 at Old Trafford on 26 September 1995 in the UEFA Cup to go through 4-2 on aggregate and York City put them out of the Coca-Cola Cup on 3 October 1995, by beating them 3-4 on aggregate)

107 GENERAL – ROUND 8
801. True
802. John Connaughton
803. Fred The Red
804. Status Quo
805. Lou Macari (Lou Macari's Fish and Chip Shop)
806. Chelsea (1-3 on 2 March 1968)
807. Blackburn Rovers (Arsenal were never in the frame)
808. Malcolm Musgrove
809. A European Championship Winner's medal (with Holland)
810. Manchester United (for Newcastle United in the FA Premier League on 21 August 1993)

108 PICTURE QUIZ – ROUND 27
1. 1952 (June 1952 from Dudley Schoolboys)
2. Three (1952-3, 1953-4 and 1954-5)
3. Cardiff City (at Old Trafford on 4 April 1953, United lost 1-4)
4. Scotland (England won 7-2)
5. 151

109 THE 1980S – ROUND 3
811. David Platt
812. Roy Aitkin
813. Peter Barnes
814. Mark Dempsey (he made his league debut against Ipswich Town at Old Trafford on 7 December 1985)
815. John Gidman
816. Canon
817. Tony Gill
818. Six (Five league – Watford, Newcastle, United, Liverpool, Tottenham Hotspur and Everton, plus one Milk Cup tie against Everton)
819. Paul McGrath and Mark Hughes
820. AFC Bournemouth (0-2 at Bournemouth on 3 January 1984)

110 IMPORTANT DATES
821. Eric Cantona joins Manchester United and helps them win their first Championship in 26 years. United enjoy unprecedented success over the following five years with Eric never out of the headlines
822. Alex Ferguson is appointed manager of Manchester United following the sacking of Ron Atkinson
823. George Best makes his debut for Manchester United standing in for Ian Moir against West Bromwich Albion at Old Trafford

824. The Munich Air Disaster. 23 people, including eight Manchester United players (Geoff Bent, Roger Byrne, Eddie Colman, Duncan Edwards, Mark Jones, David Pegg, Tommy Taylor and Billy Whelan) lost their lives when an Elizabethan jet crashed on take off at Munich Airport. United were on their way home from a European Cup Semi-Final against Red Star Belgrade

825. Manchester United defeat Bristol City 1-0 in their first ever FA Cup Final. United hold the record for the most FA Cup Final wins, winning their ninth FA Cup against Liverpool in 1996

826. Manchester United defeat Liverpool 1-0 at Wembley in the 1996 FA Cup Final and claim their second domestic double

827. Manchester United play their first-ever European tie when they beat RSC Anderlecht 2-0 in Belgium in a European Cup game. The football authorities were against English clubs participating in the competition, having banned Chelsea from taking part the previous year, but United did not heed their request

828. Matt Busby, the 'Father of Manchester United', was born

829. Manchester United become the first English club to win the European Cup, beating Benfica of Portugal 4-1 at Wembley

830. Manchester United win the Second Division Championship when they beat Southampton (a) 1-0 and make an immediate return to Division 1

111 RED DEVIL: BRYAN ROBSON
831. West Bromwich Albion
832. Five (1983, 1983 Replay, 1985, 1990 and 1990 Replay)
833. Tottenham Hotspur in the Football League Cup (at White Hart Lane on 7 October 1981)
834. False (he wasn't selected)
835. Valencia (away on 29 September 1992 in Round 1, Second Leg)
836. Manchester City (at Maine Road on 10 October 1981, 0-0 draw)
837. A dislocated shoulder
838. 12 (Eric Cantona was the new, undisputed No. 7 at United)
839. An honorary Master of Arts Degree
840. France (for England at the 1982 World Cup

Finals in Bilbao, Spain)

112: PICTURE QUIZ – ROUND 28
1. Millwall (1963)
2. Chelsea (September 1966, he cost United £55,000)
3. Manchester City (United won 1-0)
4. Eusebio (Benfica's centre-forward)
5. League Division 1 (he scored two penalties in the 1973-4 season)

113 EVENTS IN THE 1990s
841. Eric Cantona, Paul Ince, Denis Irwin and Gary Pallister
842. 0-0
843. Andrei Kanchelskis with 15 goals (Cantona 13, Cole and Hughes 12)
844. Leeds United (United beat Leeds 3-1)
845. Oldham Athletic (United won the game 2-0 at Old Trafford)
846. Bryan Robson (away to Wimbledon on 9 May 1993)
847. Gigg Lane (home of Bury)
848. Andrei Kanchelskis
849. Everton (United won 1-0)
850. False

114 1997-8 PRE-SEASON
851. Sammy McIlroy (Manager of Macclesfield Town)
852. Coventry City (David Busst's Testimonial Match, 16 May 1997)
853. John Curtis
854. Jon Macken and Ronnie Wallwork
855. Viking Stavanger
856. Five (Nicky Butt, Andy Cole, Gary Neville, Philip Neville and Paul Scholes. Teddy Sheringham was still at Spurs)
857. Paul Scholes against Italy
858. 1-1 (United lost 1-4 on penalties)
859. Michael Clegg
860. Slavia Prague (part of the deal which took Karel Poborsky to United)

115 GENERAL – ROUND 9
861. AC Milan
862. Ian McShane (of *Lovejoy* fame, his father played for United)
863. Tony Adams (1-1 draw)
864. Bobby Charlton
865. False

866. Dennis Viollet
867. 1979-80
868. Jeff Wealands
869. Shell
870. Joe Jordan, Gordon McQueen and Lou Macari

116 PICTURE QUIZ – ROUND 29
1. Alan Gowling
2. Economics
3. Stoke City (United won 4-2)
4. The British Olympic Team
5. Huddersfield Town (in June 1972 for £60,000)

117 SEASON 1997-8
871. Coventry City (at Highfield Road on 28 December 1997)
872. Dion Dublin
873. SL Benfica (Portugal)
874. Kevin Pilkington (he replaced Peter Schmeichel in the Everton game)
875. 2-2
876. Alex Norman (Paul Scholes scored the first goal)
877. Portman Road (home of Ipswich Town)
878. £27.6 million
879. Chelsea 3 Manchester United 5
880. Beckham (2), Cole (2) and Sheringham

118 RED DEVIL: TEDDY SHERINGHAM
881. £3.5 million
882. Djurgaarden and Aldershot
883. 13
884. The ZDS Cup
885. The Golden Boot (awarded to the Premiership's top goalscorer)
886. 1994-5
887. Two
888. One (for Millwall at Old Trafford on 16 September 1989, United won 5-1)
889. 28 (8 goals)
890. Yes (a Second Division Championship Winners' medal with Millwall in season 1987-8)

119 FORMER HEROES – ROUND 3
891. False (Lou Macari was born in Edinburgh, Denis Law in Aberdeen)
892. Blackpool (at Old Trafford on 26 December 1952, United won 2-1)

893. Eric Cantona (Premier League game on 19 September 1993)
894. Ray Wilkins (Bryan Robson was the Vice-Captain)
895. Duncan Edwards
896. 1990-1 (v Crystal Palace [a] on 11 May 1991)
897. Jimmy Greenhoff;
898. Lee Sharpe
899. David McCreery (2-2 draw on 27 September 1975)
900. Paul Parker

120 PICTURE QUIZ – ROUND 30
1. 1979 (August)
2. True
3. £825,000
4. One (1983)
5. Paris St Germain

FOR THE EXPERT
121 EXPERT: LEAGUE
901. Steve Coppell (206 league games between 15 January 1977 and 7 November 1981)
902. 15, 21 or 26 (Karel Poborsky was allocated No.15 for the 1996-7 season, Henning Berg was allocated No. 21 when he joined the Reds in August 1997 and Chris Casper was allocated No. 26 for the 1997-8 season)
903. Clayton Blackmore
904. 1956-7 and 1957-8
905. Bill Foulkes
906. 38 (1933-4)
907. Denis Irwin and Gary Pallister (season 1993-4)
908. Jeff Whitefoot Half-Back-Age: 16 years, 105 days
909. Billy Meredith (Forward-Age: 48 years, 285 days)
910. Willie Morgan

122 EXPERT: FA CUP
911. 14 (1909, 1948, 1957, 1958, 1963, 1976, 1977, 1979, 1983, 1985, 1990, 1994, 1995 and 1996)
912. Liverpool (on seven occasions)
913. Arthur Albiston (1977, 1983 and 1985) Bryan Robson (1983,1985 and 1990) Mark Hughes (1985, 1990 and 1994) Gary Pallister (1990, 1994 and 1996)
914. 1948 (v Blackpool), 1983 (v Brighton, Replay) and 1994 (v Chelsea)

915. Shay Brennan
916. Arthur Albiston (1977) Alan Davies (1983) Les Sealey (1990 Replay)
917. Bryan Robson (1983 [2] and 1990), Mark Hughes (1990 [2] and 1994) and Eric Cantona (1994 [2] and 1996)
918. Jimmy Delaney (he also won an FAI Cup Finalists' medal with Cork Athletic in 1956)
919. Sheffield Wednesday (Fifth Round in 1959-60, Fourth Round in 1960-1 and Fifth Round in 1961-2). United also met Sheffield Wednesday in the Fifth Round of the 1957-8 FA Cup
920. Walthamstow Avenue (Fourth Round of the 1952-3 competition, United drew 1-1 with them at Old Trafford and beat them 5-2 in the replay which was played at Arsenal Stadium)

123 EXPERT: ERIC CANTONA

921. Manchester City (Premier League game at Maine Road on 7 November 1993)
922. 'We'll never forget that night at Selhurst Park when you buried that volley against Wimbledon'
923. Blackburn Rovers (at Old Trafford on 22 January 1995)
924. Wimbledon 2, Manchester United 4 (Eric scored twice)
925. Phil Neville
926. Newcastle United (a) (4 March 1996), Queens Park Rangers (a) (16 March 1996), Arsenal (h) (20 March 1996) and Tottenham Hotspur (h) (24 March 1996)
927. None (Scorers: Beckham, Bruce, Cole, Scholes [2] and Butt)
928. Lionel Perez (Sunderland's goalkeeper)
929. Nine (4 Premierships, 2 FA Cups and 3 FA Charity Shields)
930. 80

124 EXPERT: TRIVIA – ROUND 1

931. Maine Road, Old Trafford, White Hart Lane, Goodison Park, Home Park, Plymouth (versus AS St Etienne in the ECWC 1977-8) and The Racecourse Ground, Wrexham (a Welsh side who play in the English Football League: ECWC 1991-2)
932. They all occurred in their very first home match in each competition (European Cup: 10-0 v RSC Anderlecht in 1956, European Cup Winners'Cup: 6-1 v Willem II Tilburg in 1963 and Inter Cities Fairs Cup [UEFA Cup]: 6-1 v Djurgardens IF in 1964. The RSC Anderlecht game was played at Maine Road)
933. Ferencvaros in the 1965 Inter Cities Fairs Cup Semi-Final (0-1 in second leg [a] and 1-2 in the subsequent play-off game. United won the home leg 3-2) Borussia Dortmund (0-1 in 1996-7 UEFA Champions League Semi-Final, h and a legs)
934. Bill Foulkes (52 games)
935. United were invited to participate in the 1958-9 European Cup but a joint League-FA inquiry persuaded them from taking part because they were not League Champions
936. Jackie Blanchflower and Johnny Berry
937. 22
938. Fenerbahce (Champions League game on 30 October 1996)
939. Denis Law (with 28 goals in 33 appearances)
940. Real Madrid (This first-ever home European Cup tie was in 1957 and the result 2-2)

125 EXPERT: EUROPE

941. Jack Rowley (three v West Brom [a], three v Middlesbrough [h], one v Newcastle United [h], two v Middlesbrough [a], two v Charlton [h], and three v Stoke [h] between 18 August 1951 and 8 September 1951)
942. Ryan Giggs (15 seconds v Southampton at Old Trafford in a Premier League game on 18 November 1995)
943. Shirts-Red/White quarters, Shorts Blue
944. 1993-4 (63 games: 42 League, 9 League Cup, 7 FA Cup, 4 European Cup and the FA Charity Shield)
945. Tony Coton (United paid City £500,000 for him in January 1996. The only other player that the Reds have bought directly from City is Wyn Davies who cost £60,000 in September 1972)
946. Alex Stepney, Willie Morgan and Ian Ure
947. David McCreery (he was a substitute in both the 1976 and 1977 Finals)
948. Garry Birtles (£1,250,000 from Nottingham Forest in October 1980)
949. Dion Dublin (sold to Coventry City in September 1994 for £1,950,000)
950. It was the first time that a Tribunal had decided upon a transfer fee in excess of £1million

126 EXPERT: LEAGUE CUP

951. Ron Atkinson, United's manager from 1981 to 1986, managed the winning team (Sheffield Wednesday in 1991 and Aston Villa in 1994)
952. Bryan Robson (51 games)
953. Halifax Town (they scored in both legs against United)
954. Blackmore, Hughes and Wallace
955. Burnley
956. 0-3 (Everton 1 December 1976, Spurs 25 October 1989 and York City 20 September 1995)
957. Arsenal and Leeds United (First Division Champions 1991 and 1992)
958. Aston Villa (1 -1 at home and 1-2 away. United were beaten by Aston Villa in the 1994 Coca-Cola Cup Final)
959. Paul Ince
960. Brian McClair (21 goals up to the end of the 1996-7 competition)

127 EXPERT: TRIVIA – ROUND 2

961. Denis Law (European Cup 1968-9 v Waterford [a] and he scored 4 in the home leg, ECWC 1963-4 v Willem II Tilburg [h] and Sporting Lisbon [h], Inter Cities Fairs Cup (now UEFA Cup) 1964-5 v Djurgarden IF [h])
962. Bryan Robson (West Bromwich Albion, Manchester United and Middlesbrough)
963. They won the game despite going a goal done (1979 v Liverpool, 1983 v Arsenal, 1985 v Liverpool, 1990 and 1994 v Oldham Athletic, 1995 v Crystal Palace and 1996 v Chelsea)
964. Martin Buchan, Alex Forsythe, George Graham, Lou Macari and Willie Morgan (England won 5-0)
965. Russia, Ukraine and USSR/CIS
966. Mal Donaghy (91 caps – Sammy McIlroy won 88, Jimmy Nicholl 73 and David McCreery 67. Pat Jennings is the record holder)
967. 1980-1 and 1992-3
968. Once (v Wimbledon [a] in the Fourth Round Replay on 4 February 1997. He didn't play in the 1995 Final loss to Everton as he was still serving his nine-month ban
969. 5-0 to the home side
970. He was refused a work permit by the British government because he was a non-EU national

128 EXPERT: UNITED PLAYERS

971. Remi Moses (made his United debut on 22 October 1981)
972. Nobby Stiles
973. Ronald Tudor Davies (as opposed to Ron Wyn Davies)
974. David McCreery (52 substitute appearances including two in FA Cup Finals)
975. Dion Dublin (versus Crystal Palace)
976. Ernest Taylor (February 1958-December 1958) and Terry Gibson (1986-87)
977. Ian Ure
978. Wilf McGuinness
979. Bryan Robson (12 years, 1982 to 1994)
980. Charlie Mitten (United won 7-0)

129 EXPERT: DOUBLE WINNERS

981. 27 (W 27, D 11, L 4)
982. Sheffield United 0, Manchester United 1 (Hughes)
983. May, Cole and Giggs
984. Steve Bruce (versus Reading [a])
985. Liverpool on 30 March 1994 (44,751);
986. Manchester City
987. Andy Cole and Ryan Giggs
988. Charlton Athletic (at Old Trafford, United won 3-1)
989. Two (Third Round-Sunderland and Fourth Round-Reading)
990. Leeds United 0, Manchester United 2 (Kanchelskis and Giggs)

130 EXPERT: MIXED BAG

991. Martin Buchan (1971), Gordon Strachan (1980) and Brian McClair (1987)
992. Arsenal Stadium (United beat Arsenal 5-4 on 1 February 1958)
993. Iran
994. Four times in 1892-3 (won Test Match), 1893-4 (lost Test Match), 1921-2 and 1933-4)
995. John Aston and John Aston Jnr.
996. An Open Air Market
997. Dukla Prague
998. Billy Meredith (October 1894 to October 1906 and Player/Coach July 1921 to 1924), Denis Law (March 1960 to June 1961 and July 1973 to August 1974) and Peter Barnes (July 1974 to July 1979 and January 1987 to March 1988)
999. Johnny Carey (1949)
1000. Terry Cooke

QUINDEX

Quiz
No.

OTHER TITLES AVAILABLE FROM MANCHESTER UNITED BOOKS

0 223 99178 6	*Manchester United in the Sixties* by Graham McColl	£12.99
0 233 99340 1	*Manchester United: The Insider's Guide*	£ 9.99
0 233 99359 2	*Sir Matt Busby: A Tribute* by Rick Glanvill	£14.99
0 233 99045 3	*Cantona on Cantona* by Eric Cantona	£14.99
0 233 99047 X	*Alex Ferguson: Ten Glorious Years*	£9.99
0 233 99368 1	*A Will to Win: The Manager's Diary* by Alex Ferguson with David Meek	£6.99
0 233 99362 2	*Odd Man Out: A Player's Diary* by Brian McClair	£6.99

All these books are available from your local bookshop or can be ordered direct from the publisher. Just tick the titles you require and fill in the form below.

Prices and availability are subject to change without notice.

Send to Manchester United Books Cash Sales, 76 Dean Street, London W1V 5HA.

Please send a cheque or postal order for the value of the book and add the following for postage and packaging:
UK - £1.00 for the first book, 50p for the second and 30p for each additional book up to a maximum of £3.00.
OVERSEAS including EIRE - £2.00 for the first book, £1.00 for the second and 50p for each additional book up to a maximum of £3.00.

Name

Address